For my sister, Maggie,
whose fondness for the finer things in life inspired us all.
In remembrance

Meatless Dishes in Twenty Minutes

Karen A. Levin

CB

CONTEMPORARY BOOKS

Library of Congress Cataloging-in-Publication Data

Levin, Karen A.
    Meatless dishes in twenty minutes : delicious, easy-to-prepare meals
everyone will love! / Karen A. Levin.
        p.   cm.
    Includes index.
    ISBN 0-8092-3810-1
    1. Entrées (Cookery).   2. Vegetarian cookery.   3. Quick and easy
cookery.   I. Title.
TX740.L48   1993
641.5′636—dc20   93-17574
                                                              CIP

Cover photograph by Miles Lowry
Foodstyling by Lois Hlavac

Published by Contemporary Books
A division of NTC/Contemporary Publishing Group, Inc.
4255 West Touhy Avenue, Lincolnwood (Chicago), Illinois 60712-1975 U.S.A.
Printed in the United States of America
International Standard Book Number: 0-8092-3810-1
    02 03 04 05 QP 27 26 25 24 23 22 21 20 19 18 17 16 15 14 13

Contents

✑

Introduction

Not so long ago, the average American dinner was an amazingly consistent, if rather tedious, affair. Whether it was spaghetti with meatballs on Wednesday, pot roast on Friday, or fried chicken with all the trimmings on Sunday, each evening's meal could be counted on—without question—to offer up a hefty, dense, calorie-laden helping of meat. Often, it was in the form of beef or pork; less frequently, poultry or fish. But always, in one form or another, meat was viewed as an indispensable part of our meals. Besides, what were our options? Tofu and soyburgers?

Nowadays, we've broadened our culinary horizons, and we know that there are indeed a vast number of absolutely delicious alternatives to the meat-and-potatoes fare of the past. Part of our new awareness can be traced to the increased influence of other cultures upon our own. We've learned what many people all over the world have known for centuries—that attractive, satisfying, nutritious, and, above all, *mouth-watering* meals can be prepared without a single ounce of meat.

Our health-conscious lifestyles have also drawn us toward more nutritious, lighter meals. Fresh vegetables, pastas and other grains, protein-rich legumes, tasty cheeses and eggs—all have taken a more prominent place on our tables. Supermarkets are happily keeping up with our demand for new and interesting varieties of these foods, so it's even easier to create wonderful dishes using these ingredients.

Of course, time is always a consideration when preparing any meal. Today's cook rarely has the leisure to spend hours in the kitchen. Fortunately, all of the recipes in this book require far less time than that to make. In fact, each recipe—from Quick Eggplant Parmesan to Bean and Cheese Chimichangas with Guacamole to Creamy Garlic Fettucine—can be prepared, from start to finish, in just twenty minutes or less.

While many of the recipes in this collection can be called truly vegetarian, you'll see that several do include eggs, cheeses, and even, occasionally, chicken or beef broth. I think you'll agree that this still is in keeping with today's focus on lighter, more flavorful meals. Where possible, however, alternate ingredients are included.

Enjoy!

Ingredients

Take advantage of a real time-saving boon for consumers, namely, the salad bar at your local supermarket. Most large markets throughout the country now offer an abundance of prewashed and precut vegetables and fruits to make recipe preparation a breeze. When a recipe calls for chopped bell peppers, look to see if the salad bar is offering them. Often, the yellow and red peppers are less expensive when purchased this way. Sliced mushrooms save many minutes of preparation time. Broccoli florets may be more expensive when purchased from the salad bar, but remember, there are no tough stems to discard. Prewashed and torn spinach, gourmet lettuces, and salad greens are increasingly available. Ask your produce manager where to find bottled minced garlic, minced ginger, and jalapeño peppers. These ingredients save an enormous amount of preparation time, with no sacrifice in flavor. Steadfast garlic lovers might want to use fresh garlic cloves forced through a garlic press rather than bottled minced. The ratio is 1 clove of garlic for each ½ teaspoon minced.

Stocking the Pantry

There is no substitute for a well-stocked cupboard and refrigerator when quick weekday meals are in order. Stock up on the following ingredients that appear frequently in the recipes. When you use them up, immediately put them on the next shopping list. Once or twice a week, purchase fresh produce and other perishable ingredients called for in the recipes you will be cooking throughout the week.

What to Keep in Stock

Herbs and Spices

Black peppercorns
Bottled minced ginger
Bottled minced garlic
Bottled minced jalapeño
   peppers
Dried basil, thyme, oregano,
   marjoram, and rosemary
   leaves
Dried hot red pepper flakes
Ground cumin and chili
   powder

Miscellaneous Other
Ingredients

Butter or margarine
Canned chicken and beef
   broths
Cream cheese or light cream
   cheese
Dried pastas, noodles, and
   couscous
Eggs
Niçoise, Kalamata, or ripe
   olives

Miscellaneous Other Ingredients

Onions (purchase sweet
   onions such as Vidalia,
   Walla Walla, and Maui
   when in season)
Preshredded cheeses
Quick-cooking brown,
   Arborio, basmati, long-
   grain, and boil-in-the-bag
   rice
Sour cream or light sour
   cream
Stewed tomatoes
Vegetable, chicken, and beef
   bouillon cubes

Oils and Vinegars

Balsamic and red wine
   vinegar
Extra-virgin olive oil (for
   salads)
Olive oil (for cooking)
Oriental (dark roasted) sesame
   oil
Peanut oil (for stir-fry dishes)
Vegetable oil

Sauces

Bottled pesto sauce or
   refrigerated pesto sauce
Dijon-style or country Dijon
   mustard
Hot pepper sauce
Mayonnaise or light
   mayonnaise
Prepared pizza sauce
Prepared salsa or picante
   sauce (mild, medium, or
   hot, as desired)
Prepared spaghetti sauce
Soy sauce
Tubes of tomato paste and
   pesto sauce
Worcestershire sauce

1
Vegetable, Grain, and Potato Dishes

A look at restaurant menus across the country confirms the increasing popularity of lighter, healthful meat-free dishes—particularly those that feature beans or other vegetables, grains, or potatoes as the star of the meal. The following recipes attest to the fact that meat certainly doesn't have to be the main ingredient to create a hearty, satisfying dish.

Quick Eggplant Parmesan

Eggplant has been called "the vegetarian's beef" because of its meaty texture and its ability to take on the flavors of ingredients it is prepared with. This versatile vegetable is typically associated with Mediterranean cooking, and it's the featured ingredient in this traditional southern Italian dish.

When selecting an eggplant, look for a taut, glossy skin and a green (not brown) cap. Eggplants should feel heavy for their size, and should not have any dark or soft spots.

If you do not own a microwave oven, you may heat the spaghetti sauce in a small saucepan until hot.

2 SERVINGS

1 small (about 1 pound) eggplant
1 large egg
1 tablespoon water
1 cup seasoned bread crumbs
¼ cup olive oil
¾ cup prepared spaghetti sauce (preferably
    chunky vegetable style)
⅛–¼ teaspoon dried hot red pepper flakes,
    as desired
1½ cups preshredded mozzarella cheese or
    6 ounces thinly sliced Provolone or
    mozzarella cheese
3 tablespoons grated Parmesan cheese

Cut eggplant into ¾-inch-thick slices and discard ends. Beat together egg and water in a shallow dish or pie plate. Place bread crumbs in another dish or pie plate. Dip eggplant slices in egg mixture, then in crumbs, turning and pressing to coat both sides.

Heat oil in a 12-inch skillet over medium-high heat until hot. Add eggplant slices and reduce heat to medium. Cook for 3 to 4 minutes per side or until golden brown and tender.

While eggplant is cooking, combine spaghetti sauce and pepper flakes in a microwave-safe measuring cup. Cover with plastic wrap and cook at HIGH power for 2 minutes or until heated through. Sprinkle mozzarella cheese over eggplant during last minute of cooking to melt.

Top with spaghetti sauce and Parmesan cheese, and serve immediately.

❧ *Serving suggestion:* Serve with steamed green beans and crusty French or Italian bread.

Tricolor Vegetable Fajitas

If you can find it, you may want to substitute crumbled chihuahua cheese for the Monterey Jack.

4 SERVINGS

8 7- to 8-inch flour tortillas
2 tablespoons vegetable oil
1 small red onion
1 small green bell pepper
1 small red bell pepper
1 teaspoon bottled minced garlic
1 medium yellow squash
½ cup prepared salsa or picante sauce
1 teaspoon ground cumin
½ teaspoon salt
1 cup preshredded Monterey Jack cheese
¼ cup coarsely chopped cilantro for
    garnish, if desired

Wrap tortillas in foil and place in oven. Turn heat to 350°F. Bake for 15 minutes or until heated through. While tortillas are warming, heat oil in a 10-inch skillet over medium-high heat. Cut onion lengthwise into thin strips and place in skillet. Cut bell peppers lengthwise into thin strips and place in skillet. Add garlic. Cover and reduce heat to medium. Cook for 5 minutes. Cut squash into 2-inch-long strips and stir into vegetables. Stir in salsa, cumin, and salt. Cover and cook for 5 minutes. Spoon mixture evenly down center of warm tortillas and sprinkle with cheese. Sprinkle with cilantro, if desired. Fold one end of tortilla over filling and roll up. Serve immediately.

❧ *Serving suggestion:* Serve with refried beans.

Mexican Rice Pilaf

Bottled chopped jalapeño peppers may be found in the produce section of large supermarkets. If they are not available, substitute canned or bottled pickled jalapeños, drained and chopped.

2-3 SERVINGS

1 tablespoon vegetable oil
1 medium yellow onion
1 teaspoon bottled minced garlic
1½ cups chicken, beef, or vegetable broth
1½ cups quick-cooking brown rice
2 teaspoons chili powder
1–2 teaspoons bottled minced jalapeño
    peppers, as desired
½ teaspoon ground cumin
1 red or green bell pepper
1 large tomato
1 cup preshredded Cojack or Monterey
    Jack cheese

Heat oil in a large saucepan over medium-high heat. Coarsely chop onion, add to the saucepan with garlic, and cook for 3 minutes, stirring occasionally. Stir in broth, rice, chili powder, jalapeño peppers, and cumin. Cover and bring to a boil over high heat. Reduce heat and simmer for 4 minutes. Chop bell pepper and stir into rice. Cover and simmer for 5 minutes or until liquid is absorbed. Seed and chop tomato, then stir tomato and cheese into hot cooked rice.

✱ *Serving suggestion:* Serve with warm flour or corn tortillas.

STIR-FRY SESAME VEGETABLES WITH RICE

A surprisingly short time ago, stir-fry was as foreign a cooking concept as prepackaged, minced fresh herbs and spices. Happily, both are now second nature to most American cooks—and both are used to delicious advantage in this recipe.

Although vegetable oil may be used in this recipe, I highly recommend searching out peanut oil instead. Combined with the toasted sesame seeds, it adds a wonderful nutty flavor to the dish. Peanut oil is usually shelved next to vegetable oil in the supermarket. Oriental sesame oil is located in the ethnic section of your grocery store.

Remember, the key to stir-frying is to keep the ingredients in your wok or pan moving as they cook. Continuous stirring allows for quick, even cooking.

2 SERVINGS

1½ cups chicken, beef, or vegetable broth
¾ cup long-grain white rice
1 tablespoon butter or margarine
1 tablespoon sesame seeds
8 ounces asparagus spears
1 large red or yellow bell pepper
1 large yellow onion
2 tablespoons peanut or vegetable oil
2 cups presliced mushrooms
2 teaspoons bottled minced fresh ginger
1 teaspoon bottled minced garlic
3 tablespoons soy sauce
1 tablespoon Oriental sesame oil

Combine broth, rice, and butter in a small saucepan. Cover and bring to a boil over high heat. Reduce heat to low and simmer for 16 to 17 minutes or until liquid is absorbed. While rice is cooking, heat oven or toaster oven to 350°F. Place sesame seeds on a small baking sheet. Bake for 5 to 6 minutes or until golden brown and set aside. While seeds are toasting, cut asparagus into 1-inch pieces. Cut bell pepper into 1-inch pieces. Cut onion into thin strips.

Heat oil in a large skillet or wok over medium-high heat until hot. Add asparagus, bell pepper, onion, mushrooms, ginger, and garlic. Stir-fry for 4 to 5 minutes or until vegetables are crisp-tender. Add soy sauce and stir-fry for 30 seconds. Remove from heat and stir in sesame oil and toasted sesame seeds. Serve over rice.

❧ *Serving suggestion:* Serve with melon wedges.

GRILLED VEGETABLES WITH MINTED COUSCOUS

Although is looks much like rice, couscous is actually a form of pasta made of semolina. It's extensively used in Middle Eastern cooking, and it has a delightfully subtle flavor and a texture ideal for soaking up savory juices.

The traditional method of preparing couscous is quite involved and time-consuming, and includes the use of a special two-tiered cooking apparatus called a couscoussier. *Happily, most supermarkets now stock a quick-cook form of couscous that has outstanding flavor and texture—and can be prepared in only 5 minutes.*

4 SERVINGS

4 small zucchini or yellow squash (about 1 pound)
1 red bell pepper
1 green or yellow bell pepper
½ cup bottled vinaigrette dressing, divided
1½ cups chicken, beef, or vegetable broth
2 tablespoons butter or margarine
1 cup couscous, uncooked
1 tablespoon chopped fresh mint or 1 teaspoon dried mint
Freshly ground black pepper for garnish

Prepare grill or heat broiler. Trim ends and cut zucchini in half lengthwise. Cut peppers in half lengthwise and discard stems and seeds.

Brush vegetables thoroughly with ¼ cup of the dressing. Place on grill over hot coals or broil 5 inches from heat source until browned and tender (about 10 to 12 minutes), turning once.

While vegetables are cooking, bring broth and butter to a boil in a medium saucepan. Stir in couscous, cover, and remove from heat. Let stand for 5 minutes or until liquid is absorbed. Stir in mint and transfer to a serving platter.

Cut grilled vegetables into 1-inch pieces and place over couscous. Drizzle with remaining ¼ cup dressing. Serve with freshly ground black pepper.

❧ *Serving suggestion:* Serve with wedges of Brie or Camembert cheese and crisp cracker bread.

Brown Rice with Broccoli, Cheese, and Walnuts

Broccoli is an excellent source of iron and vitamins C and A, as well as calcium and potassium. Combined with brown rice, which is rich in protein and complex carbohydrates, it makes for a hearty and nutritious meal. This dish, which also features the warm, smoky taste of Gouda cheese and the fresh crunch of walnuts, is a satisfying and substantial alternative to meat-based main courses.

If you do not own a microwave oven, steam the broccoli until tender and sprinkle with salt and pepper before topping with cheese.

4 SERVINGS

½ cup coarsely chopped walnuts
1 tablespoon butter or margarine
1 large yellow onion
½ teaspoon bottled minced garlic
1 cup quick-cooking brown rice
1 cup chicken or vegetable broth
1 bunch broccoli (about 1 pound)
½ teaspoon salt
⅛ teaspoon freshly ground black pepper
4 ounces smoked Gouda or 1 cup
    preshredded cheddar cheese

Heat oven or toaster oven to 350°F. Place walnuts on a small baking sheet and bake for 6 to 8 minutes or until toasted.

While nuts are toasting, melt butter in a medium saucepan over medium heat. Coarsely chop onion. Cook onion and garlic in butter for 3 minutes, stirring occasionally. Add rice and stir. Add broth and bring to a boil. Reduce heat to medium-low, cover, and simmer until liquid is absorbed (about 7 to 8 minutes).

While rice is cooking, cut broccoli into florets and slice stems thinly. Place in a microwave-safe casserole or dish and sprinkle with salt and pepper. Cover and cook at HIGH power for 5 to 7 minutes or until tender. While broccoli is cooking, shred cheese.

Spoon rice onto a serving platter and top with broccoli. Sprinkle walnuts over broccoli and top with cheese.

❧ *Serving suggestion:* Serve with crusty French bread.

VEGETABLE RAISIN CURRY WITH COUSCOUS

Curry powder is a wonderfully aromatic blend of highly flavored seasonings. It may be found in either the spice section or the ethnic section of the supermarket.

This curry dish is equally delicious served over rice or a baked potato. If you use Madras (hot curry powder), omit the cayenne pepper.

4 SERVINGS

¼ cup sliced almonds
2 tablespoons butter or margarine
1 large yellow onion
1 teaspoon bottled minced garlic
1 tablespoon all-purpose flour
2 teaspoons curry powder
¼ teaspoon cayenne pepper
1 16-ounce package frozen mixed
    vegetable medley such as broccoli,
    cauliflower, red bell peppers, and green
    beans
⅓ cup dark or golden raisins
½ teaspoon salt
2½ cups chicken or vegetable broth,
    divided
1 cup couscous, uncooked

Heat oven or toaster oven to 350°F. Place almonds in a single layer on a baking sheet. Bake for about 5 minutes or until golden brown.

While the almonds are baking, melt butter in a large sauce-pan over medium-high heat. Coarsely chop onion. Cook onion and garlic in butter for 2 minutes, stirring occasionally. Stir in flour, curry powder, and cayenne pepper and cook for 30 seconds, stirring constantly.

Stir in vegetables, raisins, salt, and 1 cup of the broth. Cover and bring to a boil over high heat. Reduce heat to low and continue cooking, covered, for 10 minutes, stirring occasionally.

While the curry is cooking, bring the remaining 1½ cups broth to a boil in a small saucepan. Stir in couscous and remove from heat. Cover and let stand for 5 minutes or until liquid is absorbed. Fluff with a fork. Serve vegetable curry over couscous and sprinkle with almonds.

Serving suggestion: Serve with assorted condiments such as mango chutney, chopped tomato, and shredded coconut.

CHINESE STIR-FRY BURRITOS

Traditional Oriental seasonings and ingredients take on a Mexican flair in this easy-to-make recipe.

Stir-fry sauce, plum sauce, sweet and sour sauce, and Chinese hot mustard are condiments found in the Oriental section of large supermarkets. Purchasing precut vegetables from the salad bar makes preparation even faster.

2 – 3 SERVINGS

6 7- to 8-inch flour tortillas
2 green onions with tops
4 ounces fresh shiitake mushrooms or 1½
   cups presliced mushrooms
2 tablespoons peanut or vegetable oil
⅓ cup stir-fry sauce
1 small red or yellow bell pepper or 1 cup
   prechopped bell pepper
1 teaspoon bottled minced ginger
1 teaspoon bottled minced garlic
3 cups preshredded cabbage or coleslaw
   mix (cabbage and carrots)
1 cup bean sprouts
3 tablespoons plum sauce or sweet and
   sour sauce
Chinese hot mustard for garnish, if
   desired

Wrap tortillas in foil and place in the oven, turning the temperature to 350°F. Bake for 15 minutes or until heated through.

While tortillas are baking, cut green onions into 1-inch pieces, cut pieces lengthwise into thin strips, and set aside. Discard stems from shiitake mushrooms, slice caps, and set aside.

Heat oil and stir-fry sauce in a large skillet or wok over medium-high heat until hot. Coarsely chop bell pepper and add to skillet with mushrooms, ginger, and garlic. Stir-fry for 2 minutes. Add cabbage and stir-fry for 2 minutes. Add bean sprouts and reserved green onions and stir-fry for 1 minute or until vegetables are crisp-tender.

Spread about 2 teaspoons plum sauce in the center of each warm tortilla. Spoon about ⅓ cup vegetable mixture over sauce. Fold one end of tortilla over filling and roll up. Serve with hot mustard, if desired.

❧ *Serving suggestion:* Serve with consommé or any broth-based soup.

SPEEDY STUFFED PEPPERS

Prepared in a microwave oven, these are a flavorful make-ahead alternative to the standard sandwich for lunch. They may be refrigerated and reheated in the oven or the microwave oven (cover with plastic wrap).

2 SERVINGS

2 large red, yellow, or green bell peppers
1 8-ounce can stewed tomatoes, undrained
⅓ cup quick-cooking brown rice
2 tablespoons hot water
2 green onions
½ cup frozen corn kernels
1 8-ounce can kidney or garbanzo beans
¼ teaspoon dried hot red pepper flakes
½ cup preshredded mozzarella cheese
1 tablespoon grated Parmesan cheese

Cut peppers in half lengthwise and discard seeds and membrane. Place cut-side down in a 9-inch glass baking dish or microwave-safe casserole and cover with vented plastic wrap. Cook at HIGH power for 4 minutes.

While the peppers are cooking, combine tomatoes, rice, and water in a 1-quart measuring cup or microwave-safe bowl and cover tightly with plastic wrap. Remove peppers from oven and set aside. Cook tomato mixture at HIGH power for 4 minutes.

While the tomato mixture cooks, thinly slice green onions. Place corn in a strainer and run under hot water to thaw. Add beans to the strainer and rinse under hot water.

Stir green onions, corn, beans, and pepper flakes into tomato mixture and cover with vented plastic wrap. Cook at HIGH power for 3 minutes.

Drain peppers and turn cut-side up. Spoon hot tomato mixture evenly into peppers, cover with vented plastic wrap, and cook at HIGH power for 3 to 4 minutes or until hot. Uncover and sprinkle with cheeses. Let stand for 1 to 2 minutes or until cheese is melted.

❧ *Serving suggestion:* Serve with crisp bread sticks.

RED BEANS AND RICE

This is a wonderfully flavorful meal that's a favorite of New Orleans locals as well as visitors. It's traditionally served on Sundays, partly because of long-standing custom, and partly because it can be prepared a day in advance and simply reheated before serving, which allows the cook to enjoy his or her "day of rest."

Arborio rice is a short-grained Italian rice that has a wonderful texture and flavor. If it is unavailable, substitute long-grain white rice.

2 – 3 SERVINGS

1½ cups chicken, beef, or vegetable broth
¾ cup Arborio rice, uncooked
1 tablespoon butter or margarine
2 tablespoons olive oil
1 small yellow onion
1 small green or red bell pepper
1 teaspoon bottled minced garlic
1 14½-ounce can stewed tomatoes,
   undrained
1 16-ounce can red beans, drained
1 teaspoon dried thyme
¾ teaspoon hot pepper sauce
Chopped parsley for garnish, if desired
Hot sauce for garnish, if desired

Combine broth, rice, and butter in a small saucepan. Cover and bring to a boil over high heat. Reduce heat to low and simmer for 16 to 17 minutes or until liquid is absorbed.

While rice is cooking, heat oil in a 10-inch skillet over medium-high heat. Coarsely chop onion and place in skillet. Coarsely chop bell pepper and add to skillet with garlic. Cook for 3 minutes, stirring occasionally. Stir in tomatoes, beans, thyme, and pepper sauce. Simmer uncovered for 8 to 9 minutes, stirring occasionally.

Serve over rice, with parsley and hot sauce as garnishes if desired.

✻ *Serving suggestion:* Serve with a tossed salad dressed with ranch dressing.

Vegetable Fried Rice

*This stir-fry dish combines the nutty flavor of brown rice with
the fresh taste of bell peppers, baby peas, and other vegetables*

3 – 4 SERVINGS

1½ cups quick-cooking brown rice
2 tablespoons peanut or vegetable oil
1 small yellow onion
1 small red, yellow, or green bell pepper
1 teaspoon bottled minced garlic
¼–½ teaspoon dried hot red pepper flakes,
   as desired
3 green onions with tops
3 tablespoons soy sauce
1 8-ounce can baby peas, drained, or 1
   cup frozen baby peas
2 teaspoons Oriental sesame oil
¼ cup roasted peanuts for garnish, if
   desired

Cook rice according to package directions, omitting salt. While
the rice is cooking, heat oil in a large skillet or wok over medium
heat. Coarsely chop onion and add to skillet. Coarsely chop bell
pepper and add to skillet. Add garlic and pepper flakes. Cook
vegetables 3 minutes, stirring occasionally. Thinly slice green
onions. Increase heat to medium-high and stir in hot cooked
rice, green onions, and soy sauce. Stir-fry for 1 minute. Add peas
and stir-fry for 1 minute. Remove from heat. Add sesame oil and
mix well. Sprinkle with peanuts, if desired.

❦ *Serving suggestion:* Serve with a chilled cucumber salad.

BLACK BEAN BURRITOS

Tortillas heat more evenly in the oven, but if you prefer, wrap them loosely in plastic wrap or waxed paper and microwave at HIGH power for about 1 minute or until heated.

2 SERVINGS

4 7- to 8-inch flour tortillas or 2 large
    (10-inch) flour tortillas
2 tablespoons vegetable oil
1 small yellow onion
½ red or yellow bell pepper
1 teaspoon bottled minced garlic
1 teaspoon bottled or canned minced
    jalapeño peppers
1 16-ounce can black beans, drained
3 ounces cream cheese
½ teaspoon salt
Cilantro leaves

Wrap tortillas in foil. Place in oven and turn heat to 350°F. Bake for 15 minutes or until heated through.

Heat oil in a 10-inch skillet over medium heat. Coarsely chop onion and bell pepper and place in skillet. Add garlic and jalapeños. Cook for 2 minutes, stirring occasionally. Add beans and cook for 3 minutes, stirring occasionally. Cut cream cheese into cubes and add to skillet with salt. Cook for 2 minutes stirring occasionally. Coarsely chop ¼ cup cilantro leaves and stir into mixture. Spoon mixture evenly down center of warmed tortillas. Fold one end of tortilla over filling and roll up.

❧ *Serving suggestion:* Serve with a tossed green salad.

BEAN AND CHEESE CHIMICHANGAS WITH GUACAMOLE

This is a delicious Tex-Mex version of the traditional Mexican burrito. Chimichangas are flour tortillas filled with a variety of hearty ingredients and usually deep-fried. This recipe eliminates the added fat of frying and relies on the microwave oven and the more authentically Mexican cooking technique of baking. The sour cream garnish, however, is a decidedly north-of-the-border accompaniment.

4 SERVINGS

1 16-ounce can refried beans
1½ cups preshredded cheddar cheese
⅓ cup plus 3 tablespoons prepared salsa
   or picante sauce, divided
1 teaspoon ground cumin
⅓ cup butter or margarine
8 7- to 8-inch flour tortillas
1 large ripe avocado
2 teaspoons fresh lime or lemon juice
¼ teaspoon bottled minced garlic
¼ teaspoon salt
Sour cream for garnish

Heat oven to 475°F. Combine beans, cheese, ⅓ cup of the salsa, and cumin. Mix well.

Place butter in a 10-inch glass pie plate or microwave-safe dish and cook uncovered at HIGH power for 2 to 3 minutes or until butter is melted. Dip one side of each tortilla in butter and place butter-side down on another plate or paper plate. Spoon ⅓ cup bean mixture into the center of each tortilla and fold the two outer edges in over filling. Roll up envelope-fashion and place seam-side down in a 13" X 9" baking dish. Bake for 12 minutes or until golden brown.

While the tortillas are baking, peel and seed avocado, cut into chunks, and place in a small bowl. Mash with a fork to desired consistency. Stir in remaining 3 tablespoons salsa, lime juice, garlic, and salt, mixing well. Serve chimichangas with guacamole and sour cream.

❧ *Serving suggestion:* Serve with vegetable soup.

TOSTADOS CON FRIJOLES

This might be described as the Mexican version of an open-face sandwich.

4 SERVINGS

1 16-ounce can refried beans
⅓ cup sour cream
¼ cup plus 2 tablespoons prepared salsa
    or picante sauce, divided
1 teaspoon ground cumin
Lettuce leaves
1 large tomato
2 green onions with tops
3 tablespoons vegetable oil
4 7- to 8-inch corn or flour tortillas
1 cup preshredded cheddar cheese

Combine beans, sour cream, 2 tablespoons salsa, and cumin in a medium saucepan. Cook uncovered over low heat for 10 minutes, stirring occasionally. While the beans are cooking, thinly slice enough lettuce leaves to measure 1½ cups. Seed and chop tomato. Thinly slice green onions. Heat oil in a 10-inch skillet over medium-high heat until hot but not smoking. Fry tortillas one at a time in hot oil until browned and crisp, about 1 minute per side. (If tortillas are browning too fast, reduce heat to medium.) Transfer tortillas to paper towels to drain, then place on serving plates and top with bean mixture and remaining ¼ cup salsa. Sprinkle cheese evenly over beans and top with lettuce, tomato, and green onions.

꙰ *Serving suggestion:* Serve with fresh pineapple spears.

BARBECUED BEAN CASSEROLE

This is a tasty, filling dish that's perfect for informal summer get-togethers or chilly winter nights.

4 SERVINGS

1 tablespoon vegetable oil
1 large yellow onion
1 teaspoon bottled minced garlic
1 large red or green bell pepper
1 18-ounce jar oven-baked beans,
    undrained
1 16-ounce can dark red kidney beans,
    drained
1 16-ounce can butter beans, drained
¾ cup packed light brown sugar
½ cup catsup
2 tablespoons Dijon-style mustard
1 tablespoon cider or distilled vinegar
Sour cream for garnish, if desired

Heat oil in a large saucepan over medium heat. While oil is heating, peel and coarsely chop onion. Sauté onion and garlic in oil for 3 minutes, stirring occasionally.

While onion and garlic are cooking, coarsely chop bell pepper and set aside. Add beans, brown sugar, catsup, mustard, and vinegar to saucepan. Mix well and bring to a boil. Stir bell pepper into beans and simmer, uncovered, for 8 to 10 minutes, stirring frequently. Transfer to individual serving bowls and garnish with sour cream, if desired.

❧ *Serving suggestion:* Serve with chips and a tossed green salad.

BEAN AND CHEESE ENCHILADAS

Pinto beans are a staple in Mexican households. Here they're used to create a fairly traditional south-of-the-border meal.

4 SERVINGS

1 16-ounce can pinto beans
½ cup prepared salsa or picante sauce,
    divided
1 teaspoon ground cumin
½ teaspoon bottled minced garlic
2 cups preshredded Cojack or cheddar
    cheese, divided
8 7- to 8-inch flour tortillas
1 10-ounce can enchilada sauce
Chopped cilantro for garnish
Sour cream for garnish

Drain and rinse beans and transfer to a medium bowl. Add ¼ cup of the salsa, cumin, and garlic and mix well. Stir in 1 cup of the cheese. Spoon ⅓ cup of the mixture down center of each tortilla, roll tortillas up, and place seam-side down in an 11″ × 7″ glass baking dish or 1½-quart shallow microwave-safe casserole dish. Combine remaining ¼ cup salsa and enchilada sauce and spoon evenly over tortillas. Cover with waxed paper and microwave at HIGH power for 5 minutes. Remove waxed paper and sprinkle with remaining 1 cup cheese. Cover with waxed paper and microwave at HIGH power for 4 to 5 minutes or until heated through. Sprinkle with cilantro and serve with sour cream.

✎ *Serving suggestion:* Serve with a cold marinated vegetable salad.

TEX-MEX POTATOES

These highly seasoned potatoes are best served in shallow bowls to catch all the flavorful sauce.

4 SERVINGS

4 medium baking potatoes
1 tablespoon vegetable oil
1 medium yellow onion
1 large green or red bell pepper
1 teaspoon bottled minced garlic
1 15- to 16-ounce can chili beans in spicy
    sauce, undrained
1 tablespoon Worcestershire sauce
½ teaspoon bottled or canned minced
    jalapeño peppers, if desired
1 cup preshredded Monterey Jack cheese
Sour cream for garnish

Scrub potatoes and prick in several places with the tip of a sharp knife. Place on a paper towel in the microwave oven and cook at HIGH power for 8 minutes. Turn and rotate potatoes and continue to cook at HIGH power for 8 to 10 minutes or until tender.

While potatoes are cooking, heat oil in a 10-inch skillet over medium heat. Coarsely chop onion and bell pepper and place in skillet. Add garlic. Cook vegetables for 3 minutes, stirring occasionally. Add beans, Worcestershire sauce, and, if desired, jalapeño peppers. Reduce heat to low. Cover and simmer for 5 to 6 minutes. Split potatoes and top with bean mixture. Sprinkle with cheese and serve with sour cream.

❧ *Serving suggestion:* Serve with a tossed green salad.

POLENTA WITH MUSHROOM MARINARA SAUCE

Polenta is an Italian dish that can be made with semolina, farina, chestnut meal, or other meal. This recipe calls for cornmeal, which is perhaps the most commonly used. Topped with a flavorful mushroom sauce, it's a quick and easy dish with a distinctively European flair.

This foolproof polenta is made in the microwave oven while the sauce simmers on the range top. Using a wire whisk keeps the polenta from lumping.

2 SERVINGS

1 14-ounce can chicken broth (see note)
½ cup cornmeal
½ cup preshredded mozzarella cheese
1 tablespoon olive oil
1 small yellow onion
2 cups (6 ounces) presliced mushrooms
1 teaspoon bottled minced garlic
1 14- to 15-ounce jar prepared spaghetti
    sauce
3 tablespoons dry red wine, if desired
¼ teaspoon dried hot red pepper flakes
Grated Parmesan cheese for garnish

Whisk together broth and cornmeal in a medium microwave-safe bowl. Cover with waxed paper and cook at HIGH power for 5 minutes. Whisk until smooth. Cover with waxed paper and continue cooking at HIGH power for 3 minutes. Whisk until smooth. Cover with waxed paper and continue cooking at HIGH power for 3 to 4 minutes or until polenta is very thick. Whisk in mozzarella cheese. Cover and let stand until serving time.

While polenta is cooking, heat oil in a 10-inch skillet over medium-high heat. Chop onion and place in skillet. Add mushrooms and garlic and cook for 3 minutes, stirring occasionally. Add spaghetti sauce, wine, if desired, and pepper flakes. Simmer uncovered over medium-low heat for 10 minutes, stirring occasionally.

Spread polenta evenly over center of two dinner plates. Spoon sauce over polenta and sprinkle with Parmesan cheese.

❧ *Serving suggestion:* Serve with a Caesar salad.

❧ *Note: If desired, substitute 1¾ cups water plus ½ teaspoon salt for chicken broth.*

2
Egg and Cheese Dishes

ℐ

Probably the most economical of all meatless dishes are those that feature eggs as a key ingredient. Because they cook so quickly, egg dishes are a speedy, flavorful choice for rushed weekday meals. Many supermarkets now carry farm-fresh eggs, which provide a preservative-free alternative for health-conscious cooks.

Cheese is the most-used ingredient in meatless dishes around the world. Now that there is a wide variety of delicious, quality cheeses in almost any grocery store or deli, meatless meals that feature cheese can be extremely versatile as well as easy. You can also take advantage of time-saving packaged, preshredded cheeses for dishes prepared in a snap.

VEGETABLE OMELET WITH SMOKED GOUDA

The rich, smoky flavor of Gouda blends deliciously with bell peppers and onions in this omelet.

2 SERVINGS

2 tablespoons butter or margarine, divided
1 small yellow onion
½ large red or green bell pepper
4 large eggs
2 tablespoons milk or water
¾ teaspoon salt, divided
⅛ teaspoon freshly ground black pepper
2 ounces Gouda or Swiss cheese,
    preferably smoked
Dijon-style mustard for garnish, if desired

Melt 1 tablespoon of the butter in a 10-inch skillet with sloped sides over medium heat. Coarsely chop onion and place in skillet. Coarsely chop bell pepper and add to skillet. Cook for 4 to 5 minutes or until vegetables are crisp-tender, stirring occasionally.

While vegetables are cooking, beat eggs with milk, ½ teaspoon of the salt, and pepper. Shred cheese and set aside. Sprinkle remaining ¼ teaspoon of the salt over vegetables, transfer to bowl, and set aside.

Melt remaining 1 tablespoon butter in same skillet over medium-high heat. Swirl butter around edges of skillet to prevent omelet from sticking. When butter is bubbly, add egg mixture.

Cook for 2 minutes or until eggs begin to set on bottom. Gently lift edges of omelet with a spatula to allow uncooked portion of eggs to flow to edges and set. Continue cooking for 2 to 3 minutes or until center is almost set. Sprinkle cheese over eggs and spoon vegetables down center.

Using a large spatula, fold one edge over the filling and slide onto a warm serving platter. Serve with mustard, if desired.

✤ *Serving suggestion:* Serve with pumpernickel or rye toast.

CHEESE AND AVOCADO OMELET

Cojack cheese is a combination of Colby and Monterey Jack cheese. If it is unavailable in the preshredded form, substitute preshredded mild cheddar cheese.

2 SERVINGS

4 large eggs
2 tablespoons milk or water
¼ teaspoon salt
⅛ teaspoon freshly ground black pepper
1 ripe avocado
1 tablespoon butter or margarine
¾ cup preshredded Cojack cheese
½ cup prepared salsa or picante sauce

Beat eggs with milk, salt, and pepper. Dice avocado and set aside. Heat butter over medium-high heat in a 10-inch skillet with sloped sides. Swirl butter around edges of skillet to prevent omelet from sticking. When butter is bubbly, add egg mixture. Cook for 2 minutes or until eggs begin to set on bottom. Gently lift edges of omelet with a spatula to allow uncooked portion of eggs to flow to edges and set. Continue cooking for 3 minutes or until center is almost set. Sprinkle diced avocado and cheese evenly over omelet, leaving a 1-inch-wide border around the edge. Using a large spatula, fold one edge over the filling and slide onto a warm serving platter. Heat salsa in same skillet over high heat. Pour over center of omelet and serve.

❧ *Serving suggestion:* Serve with warm corn muffins or cornbread.

HUEVOS RANCHEROS

This is a terrific, easy meal to serve any time of the day.

2 SERVINGS

¼ *cup vegetable oil*
2 *7- to 8-inch corn tortillas*
1 *tablespoon butter or margarine*
4 *large eggs*
⅓ *cup prepared salsa or picante sauce*
2 *tablespoons catsup*
½ *cup preshredded cheddar or Monterey*
  Jack or Cojack cheese
Sliced green onions or chopped cilantro for
  garnish, if desired

Heat oil in a 10-inch skillet over medium-high heat until hot but not smoking. Fry tortillas in oil until lightly browned and crisp, about 1 minute per side. Transfer to paper towels to drain. Pour off oil and melt butter in same skillet over medium heat. Fry eggs in butter sunny-side up or over easy, as desired. Place 2 eggs on each tortilla. Combine salsa and catsup in same skillet and heat over high heat until hot. Pour over eggs and sprinkle with cheese. Sprinkle with onions, if desired.

✌ *Serving suggestion:* Serve with sliced avocado and sliced tomatoes.

ASPARAGUS EGGS BENEDICT

Thanks to this foolproof blender hollandaise sauce, this dish is ready in under twenty minutes. Be sure the butter is bubbly and hot enough to "cook" the raw egg yolks.

If a microwave oven is not available, steam the asparagus until tender (about 5 minutes) and melt the butter in a small saucepan.

2 SERVINGS

12 thin asparagus spears (about 4 ounces)
4 large eggs
3 large egg yolks
1 tablespoon fresh lemon juice
¼ teaspoon salt
Pinch of cayenne pepper
⅓ cup butter
2 whole wheat or sourdough English
   muffins

Fill a medium saucepan or wide deep skillet ¾ full with hot tap water. Bring to a boil over high heat. Reduce heat to maintain a gentle boil.

Trim off and discard woody ends of asparagus. Place asparagus in a shallow microwave-safe casserole dish, cover with vented plastic wrap, and cook at HIGH power for 1½ to 2½ minutes or until crisp-tender. Cover tightly and set aside in a warm place.

Break whole eggs, one at a time, into a small dish. Slip eggs into simmering water. Cook about 3 minutes for soft-set eggs, or until cooked as desired.

While eggs are cooking, place egg yolks in a blender container. Add lemon juice, salt, and cayenne pepper. Place butter in a microwave-safe measuring cup and cook at HIGH power until melted and bubbly, about 1 to 1½ minutes. With blender running, pour hot butter in a stream through the hole in the lid. Blend for 30 seconds or until sauce has thickened.

Split and toast English muffins. Place 3 asparagus spears over each muffin half. Using a slotted spoon, place poached eggs over asparagus. Spoon sauce over eggs.

ℱ *Serving suggestion:* Serve with a fresh fruit salad or melon wedges.

POTATO FRITTATA

A frittata is the Italian version of a crustless quiche. It cooks very quickly by starting on top of the range and finishing under a broiler. If your skillet is not ovenproof, wrap the handle with heavy-duty aluminum foil before broiling. The frozen potatoes may be thawed in a microwave-safe bowl in the microwave oven on HIGH power for 2 to 3 minutes.

4 SERVINGS

3 tablespoons butter or margarine
2 cups (8 ounces) frozen ready-to-cook
    hash brown potatoes with peppers and
    onions (O'Brien style), thawed
5 large eggs
3 tablespoons half-and-half or milk
¾ teaspoon salt
¼ teaspoon freshly ground black pepper
¾ cup preshredded cheddar cheese
Sour cream for garnish, if desired

Melt butter in a 10-inch ovenproof skillet over medium-high heat. Swirl butter up the sides of the pan to prevent sides of frittata from sticking. Add potatoes to skillet and cook for 3 minutes, stirring occasionally.

While potatoes are cooking, heat broiler. Beat eggs with half-and-half, salt, and pepper, mixing well. Reduce heat under skillet to medium. Pour egg mixture over potatoes and stir gently to combine. Cover and cook for 6 minutes or until eggs are set around the edges. (Center will be wet.)

Sprinkle cheese evenly over frittata. Transfer to the broiler so surface of skillet is 4 to 5 inches from heat source. Broil for 2 minutes or until cheese is melted and eggs are set in center.

Cut into wedges and serve with sour cream, if desired.

✄ *Serving suggestion:* Serve with toasted English muffins and jam.

BROCCOLI-PEPPER FRITTATA

For speedy preparation, purchase broccoli florets and diced bell pepper from the salad bar at large supermarkets.

4 SERVINGS

2 tablespoons butter or margarine
2 cups (about 4 ounces) small broccoli
   florets
½ cup coarsely chopped red or green bell
   pepper
2 green onions with tops
5 large eggs
¼ cup half-and-half or milk
½ teaspoon salt
¼ teaspoon freshly ground black pepper
½ cup grated Asiago or Parmesan cheese

Melt butter in a 10-inch ovenproof skillet over medium heat. Stir in broccoli and bell pepper, cover, and steam for 5 minutes, stirring once. While vegetables are steaming, heat broiler. Thinly slice green onions. Beat eggs with half-and-half in a medium bowl. Stir in green onions, salt, and pepper. Uncover skillet and stir in egg mixture to combine. Cover and cook for about 5 minutes over medium-low heat or until eggs are set around the edges. (Center will be wet.)

Sprinkle cheese evenly over frittata. Transfer to the broiler, 4 to 5 inches from heat source. Broil for 2 minutes or until cheese is melted and eggs are set in center. Cut into wedges.

❧ *Serving suggestion:* Serve with a tossed green salad and crusty rolls.

CHEESY EGG AND VEGGIE TACOS

Tacos are a favorite finger food, whether filled with beans, guacamole, or quick-cooking eggs and vegetables, as this recipe proves.

2 SERVINGS

4 7- to 8-inch flour tortillas or 4 prepared
   taco shells
1 green onion with top
½ small red or green bell pepper
2 tablespoons butter or margarine
4 large eggs
½ teaspoon salt
⅓ cup prepared salsa or picante sauce
½ cup preshredded sharp cheddar cheese

Wrap flour tortillas in foil or place taco shells on a baking sheet. Place in oven and turn temperature to 350°F. Bake flour tortillas for 10 minutes or taco shells for 5 minutes until heated through. While tortillas are heating, thinly slice green onion. Cut bell pepper into ¼-inch pieces. Melt butter in a 10-inch skillet over medium heat. Cook bell pepper in butter for 2 minutes, stirring occasionally. Beat eggs and stir in green onions and salt. Add egg mixture to skillet. Cook until eggs are soft-set, stirring occasionally. Add salsa and heat through. Spoon eggs into warm tortillas or taco shells and sprinkle with cheese.

❧ *Serving suggestion:* Serve with refried beans.

QUESADILLAS

For even quicker preparation, purchase chopped onion and chopped red or green bell pepper from the salad bar located in the produce section of most large supermarkets.

2 SERVINGS

2 tablespoons butter or margarine, divided
1 small yellow onion
1 small red or green bell pepper
1 teaspoon bottled minced garlic
4 7- to 8-inch flour tortillas
1 cup preshredded Cojack or cheddar
   cheese
2 tablespoons chopped cilantro, if desired

Melt 1 tablespoon of the butter in a 10-inch skillet over medium heat. Chop onion and place in skillet. Chop bell pepper and add to skillet with garlic. Cook vegetables for 4 to 5 minutes or until tender, stirring occasionally. While vegetables are cooking, sprinkle cheese over half of each tortilla, leaving a ½-inch-wide border around the edges. Top with cooked vegetables and sprinkle with cilantro, if desired. Fold tortillas in half over filling and press lightly to seal. Melt ½ tablespoon of the butter in the same skillet, add 2 folded tortillas, and cook for 2 minutes on each side or until golden brown. Repeat with remaining ½ tablespoon butter and remaining 2 tortillas.

✒ *Serving suggestion:* Serve with sour cream, diced avocado, and prepared salsa or picante sauce for topping the quesadillas.

CHEDDAR CORN PANCAKES

Pancakes are always a breakfast favorite, but these are substantial enough to satisfy dinnertime hunger as well.

4 SERVINGS

2 tablespoons butter or margarine
2 large eggs
¾ cup milk
1 cup yellow cornmeal
½ cup all-purpose flour
1 tablespoon sugar
2 teaspoons baking powder
½ teaspoon salt
1 8-ounce can whole kernel corn, drained
½ cup preshredded sharp cheddar cheese
Pure maple syrup (heated, if desired)

Melt butter in a large nonstick skillet and set aside to cool slightly. Beat eggs in a mixing bowl. Beat in milk. Add cornmeal, flour, sugar, baking powder, and salt and mix lightly. Add corn, cheese, and melted butter from skillet and mix just until combined. (Overmixing causes pancakes to become tough.)

Heat the same skillet over medium-high heat until hot. Drop batter by ¼ cupfuls into hot skillet and cook until golden brown, for about 2 minutes per side. Repeat with remaining batter. Serve with syrup.

❧ *Serving suggestion:* Serve with a fresh fruit salad.

Egg Foo Yung with Mushroom Sauce

This Oriental favorite is the perfect meal for busy days. For a spicier version, add ¼ teaspoon dried hot red pepper flakes to the egg mixture.

2 SERVINGS

4 large eggs
1 green onion with top
¾ cup fresh or drained canned bean
    sprouts
3 tablespoons soy sauce, divided
2 tablespoons peanut or vegetable oil,
    divided
2 cups presliced mushrooms
1 cup chicken or beef broth (see note)
4 teaspoons cornstarch

Beat eggs in a medium bowl. Thinly slice green onion and reserve 1 tablespoon of the top for garnish. Add remaining onion, bean sprouts, and 1 tablespoon soy sauce to egg mixture and mix well. Heat 1 tablespoon of the oil in a large nonstick skillet over medium-high heat until hot. For each pancake, drop ¼ cup egg mixture into hot oil. (Egg mixture will run—do not crowd skillet.) Cook for 1 to 2 minutes or until bottoms of cakes are set. Turn and cook for 1 to 2 minutes or until cooked through. Transfer to a warm serving plate and keep warm. Repeat with remaining egg mixture.

Heat remaining 1 tablespoon oil in same skillet. Add mush-rooms and remaining 2 tablespoons soy sauce to skillet and cook over medium heat for 3 minutes, stirring occasionally. Combine broth and cornstarch and mix until smooth. Add to skillet and cook, stirring constantly until sauce has thickened. Pour over egg foo yung and sprinkle with reserved onion.

❧ *Serving suggestions:* Serve with a spinach salad with sesame-soy dressing.

❧ *Note: Because the broth in this recipe greatly contributes to the flavor of the dish, vegetable broth (which does not have as much flavor) is not recommended. If, however, you prefer, you may use vegetable broth instead of chicken or beef.*

Quick Cheese Blintzes

Packaged prepared crepes may be found in specialty stores or in some supermarkets in the fresh produce section. If unavailable, prepare crepes as directed on pancake mix package when time permits and place between sheets of waxed paper in heavy plastic storage bag. The crepes will keep refrigerated up to 3 days or frozen up to 3 months. They thaw quickly at room temperature.

2 SERVINGS

1 15-ounce container ricotta cheese
¼ cup powdered sugar
1 teaspoon vanilla
⅛ teaspoon ground nutmeg
8 packaged prepared or homemade 8-inch-
   diameter crepes
3 tablespoons butter or margarine, divided
Strawberry preserves for garnish
Sour cream for garnish

Combine cheese, sugar, vanilla, and nutmeg in a food processor fitted with the steel blade. Process until fairly smooth. (Mixture may be combined by hand in a medium bowl, but will retain a more grainy texture.) Spoon ¼ cup cheese mixture in center of each crepe. Fold opposite ends of crepe over cheese and roll up envelope-style. Melt 1½ tablespoons of the butter in a 10-inch skillet over medium heat until bubbly. Add 4 blintzes to skillet and cook for 1 to 2 minutes per side or until golden brown. Repeat with remaining 1½ tablespoons butter and 4 blintzes. Serve warm with preserves and sour cream.

❧ *Serving suggestion:* Serve with chilled applesauce.

3

Hearty Salads

❧

Once served only on the dog days of a hot summer, main-dish salads are making a dramatic comeback in American cuisine. There is now a tantalizing variety of seasonal and warm salads to be enjoyed throughout the year.

Purchasing prewashed, precut greens and vegetables will make preparation even speedier for the time-pressed cook. An increasing number of grocers now offer prepackaged, washed spinach and salad greens, as well as presliced mushrooms and other popular veggies. Nothing, of course, beats a bountiful salad bar, which is also becoming a staple of the local produce department.

MEDITERRANEAN-STYLE SALAD

For this recipe, be sure to take advantage of prewashed, packaged salad greens and gourmet greens available in most supermarkets. Otherwise, choose greens from the salad bar in the produce section of your supermarket. If fresh basil is unavailable, add 1 teaspoon dried basil to the salad dressing.

2 SERVINGS

1 small red or yellow bell pepper
½ cup Kalamata or pitted ripe olives
4 cups packed torn assorted salad greens
  such as red leaf, spinach, romaine, or
  curly endive
½ cup prepared garlic croutons
½ cup crumbled feta or goat cheese
¼ cup packed shredded fresh basil leaves
3 tablespoons extra-virgin olive oil
1½ tablespoons balsamic or red wine
  vinegar
½ teaspoon bottled minced garlic
¼ teaspoon salt
¼ teaspoon sugar
¼ teaspoon freshly ground black pepper

Cut bell pepper into short, thin strips or coarsely chop. To seed olives, strike with a mallet or heavy can to split olive and discard seed. Combine bell pepper, olives, greens, croutons, cheese, and basil in a large bowl. Combine oil, vinegar, garlic, salt, sugar, and black pepper and mix well. Add to greens and toss well.

❧ *Serving suggestion:* Serve with crusty Italian bread.

VEGETABLE COBB SALAD

Keep hard-cooked eggs in the refrigerator up to one week. They are a tasty addition to any salad.

4 SERVINGS

4 cups packed shredded romaine lettuce
   leaves
1 8-ounce can garbanzo or red kidney
   beans
1 large or 2 medium ripe tomatoes
1 large ripe avocado
½ cup (2 ounces) crumbled bleu cheese
½ cup drained canned julienned or diced
   beets
⅓ cup drained canned sliced ripe olives
2 hard-cooked eggs, peeled and diced, if
   desired
⅓ cup olive or vegetable oil
3 tablespoons red wine vinegar
½ teaspoon salt
¼ teaspoon sugar
¼ teaspoon freshly ground black pepper

Arrange lettuce on a large serving platter or in a large salad bowl. Rinse and drain beans. Seed and dice tomato. Peel, seed, and dice avocado. Arrange beans, tomato, avocado, cheese, beets, olives, and eggs, if desired, in rows over lettuce. Combine oil, vinegar, salt, sugar, and pepper and mix well with a fork. Drizzle evenly over salad and toss well.

❧ *Serving suggestion:* Serve with pecan or banana muffins.

BLACK BEAN SALAD WITH HEARTS OF PALM

Cumin and lime juice are a delicious combination, as this recipe proves. If marinated hearts of palm are not available in your market, substitute marinated artichoke hearts.

2–3 SERVINGS

1 16-ounce can black beans
1 cup frozen corn kernels
1 6- to 7-ounce jar marinated hearts of
    palm
½ small red onion
1 large ripe avocado
¼ cup extra-virgin olive oil
¼ cup prepared salsa or picante sauce
2–3 tablespoons fresh lime juice, as
    desired
1 teaspoon ground cumin
Lettuce or spinach leaves
Chopped cilantro for garnish, if desired

Drain and rinse beans. Rinse corn under warm water until thawed, about 1 minute, or microwave at HIGH power for about 1 minute or until thawed. Drain hearts of palm. Finely chop red onion. Peel, seed, and dice avocado. Combine beans, corn, hearts of palm, onion, and avocado in a large bowl. Combine oil, salsa, lime juice, and cumin and mix well. Add to salad and toss well. Serve on lettuce leaves and sprinkle with cilantro, if desired.

❧ *Serving suggestion:* Serve with corn bread or corn muffins.

SOUTHWESTERN-STYLE SALAD

This is similar to a taco salad, without the shell. Served with tortilla chips, it's a simple—but filling—meal.

4 SERVINGS

1 16-ounce can pinto or red kidney beans
2 green onions with tops
1 small red bell pepper
1 cup preshredded Monterey Jack or
    Cojack cheese
¼ cup coarsely chopped cilantro
¼ cup prepared salsa or picante sauce
¼ cup bottled Italian dressing
1 tablespoon fresh lime juice
½ teaspoon ground cumin
Romaine lettuce leaves
Lime wedges for garnish, if desired

Rinse and drain beans. Thinly slice green onions. Coarsely chop bell pepper. Combine beans, onions, bell pepper, cheese, and cilantro in a large bowl. Combine salsa, dressing, lime juice, and cumin and mix well. Add to bowl and toss salad. Serve on lettuce leaves and garnish with lime wedges, if desired.

✤ *Serving suggestion:* Serve with tortilla chips.

WILTED SPINACH AND THREE BEAN SALAD

Wilted spinach was a very popular dish in the fifties. This recipe omits the cholesterol-laden bacon called for in the traditional version and adds a healthy amount of nutrient-rich beans to bring this dish into the health-conscious nineties.

4 SERVINGS

1 8-ounce can garbanzo or butter beans
1 8-ounce can red kidney beans
1 cup drained canned black beans
6 cups packed prewashed spinach leaves
⅓ cup olive oil
1 small red onion
1 teaspoon bottled minced garlic
3 tablespoons balsamic vinegar
½ teaspoon salt
Freshly ground black pepper for garnish

Rinse and drain beans. Discard stems of spinach leaves and tear leaves into bite-sized pieces. Combine beans and spinach in a large bowl. Heat oil in a 10-inch skillet over medium heat. Coarsely chop onion and place in skillet. Add garlic and cook for 3 to 4 minutes or until onion is crisp-tender, stirring occasionally. Remove from heat and stir in vinegar and salt. Immediately pour over spinach and toss well. Serve with pepper.

❧ *Serving suggestion:* Serve with warm croissants.

RAVIOLI ANTIPASTO SALAD

This salad is served at room temperature just as the antipasto courses are served in Italy.

4 SERVINGS

1 9-ounce package refrigerated cheese-,
  garlic-and-cheese-, or
  herb-and-cheese-filled ravioli, uncooked
1 6-ounce jar marinated artichoke hearts
1 large ripe tomato
½ cup Kalamata or pitted ripe olives
4 ounces provolone or mozzarella cheese
Bottled Italian dressing
Freshly ground black pepper for garnish

Cook ravioli according to package directions. While ravioli are cooking, drain artichoke hearts, reserving marinade. Coarsely chop artichoke hearts. Seed and coarsely chop tomato. To seed olives, strike with a mallet or heavy can to split olive and discard seed. Cut cheese into ½-inch-thick pieces. Add enough dressing to reserved marinade to equal ½ cup, or discard marinade and use ½ cup dressing. Combine artichoke hearts, tomato, olives, cheese, and dressing in a large bowl. Drain ravioli and rinse under cold water for 1 minute. Add to salad and toss well. Serve with pepper.

❧ *Serving suggestion:* Serve with crisp bread sticks.

PANZANELLA SALAD WITH BEANS

Panzanella is a traditional Italian bread and tomato salad. The addition of beans makes it hearty enough for a main course.

This salad is best when made with vine-ripened tomatoes, but if they are out of season, purchase hydroponic or hothouse tomatoes.

2 – 3 SERVINGS

1 small (about 3-ounce) French bread
    baguette
4 tablespoons extra-virgin olive oil,
    divided
½ teaspoon bottled minced garlic
2 large very ripe tomatoes (about 1
    pound)
1 16- to 19-ounce can cannellini or great
    northern beans
¼ cup finely chopped red onion
2 tablespoons chopped fresh basil or 1
    teaspoon dried basil
2 tablespoons balsamic vinegar
¼ teaspoon salt
¼ teaspoon freshly ground black pepper
¼ cup preshredded Asiago cheese or grated
    Parmesan cheese

Heat broiler. Cut bread into ¾-inch cubes and transfer to a jelly roll pan. Combine 2 tablespoons of the oil with garlic and drizzle evenly over bread. Toss lightly to coat. Broil 4 to 5 inches from heat source for 3 minutes or until toasted, stirring once after 2 minutes.

While bread is broiling, cut tomatoes in half. Working over a strainer placed in a bowl, squeeze the seeds and juice from tomato halves into the strainer. Press on the seeds to extract juices and discard seeds. Cut tomatoes into ¾-inch-thick pieces and add to bowl with juices. Drain and rinse beans. Add beans, onion, basil, remaining 2 tablespoons oil, vinegar, salt, and pepper to bowl and toss. Add toasted bread and toss lightly. Sprinkle with cheese.

❦ *Serving suggestion:* Serve with vegetable soup.

GORGONZOLA, PEAR, AND WALNUT SALAD

Walnut oil has a wonderful, nutty aroma and taste and is well worth searching out in your supermarket. If it is unavailable, substitute extra-virgin olive oil.

2 SERVINGS

½ cup walnut halves or large pieces
1 large ripe pear
4 cups packed assorted bitter salad greens
1 cup (about 4 ounces) crumbled
    Gorgonzola or Stilton cheese
¼ cup walnut oil
1½ tablespoons fresh lemon juice
1 teaspoon sugar
1 teaspoon Dijon-style mustard
¼ teaspoon salt
⅛ teaspoon freshly ground black pepper

Heat oven to 350°F. Place walnuts on a small baking sheet and bake for 6 to 8 minutes or until toasted. While walnuts are toasting, dice pear into ½-inch-thick cubes.

Remove toasted walnuts from oven and let cool. Combine greens, pear, and cheese in a large bowl. Combine oil, lemon juice, sugar, mustard, salt, and pepper, mixing well with a fork. Add to greens with cooled walnuts and toss well.

✂ *Serving suggestion:* Serve with warmed French rolls.

4
Substantial Sandwiches

❧

Often thought of as strictly luncheon fare, sandwiches can be a great main course for any meal. The exotic breads now widely available from good bakeries and grocers make it easy to make sandwiches a special, change-of-pace dinner—and what could be easier to eat on the run than a breakfast sandwich, filled with fresh, healthful ingredients, to start the day?

MEATLESS MONTE CRISTO SANDWICHES

Honey mustard may be found in the condiment section of your supermarket. If unavailable, substitute Dijon-style mustard.

2 SERVINGS

4 large (about 6" × 3") oval slices
   sourdough bread
Prepared honey mustard
2 large (1 ounce each) slices Swiss cheese
2 eggs
¼ cup milk
1–2 tablespoons butter or margarine
Raspberry or strawberry preserves for
   garnish

Spread one side of each slice of bread lightly with honey mustard. Place cheese on 2 slices bread, folding to fit. Close sandwich with remaining bread, mustard-side down.

Beat eggs in a pie plate or large shallow bowl. Add milk and beat well. Melt butter in a large skillet over medium heat. Dip each sandwich in egg mixture for about 30 seconds per side or until well coated. Fry sandwiches in butter for about 3 to 4 minutes per side until golden brown. Serve immediately with preserves.

🌿 *Serving suggestion:* Serve with vegetable soup.

LAYERED ITALIAN SANDWICHES

Pickled jardiniere vegetables may be found in the olive and pickle section of your supermarket. Choose hot or mild jardiniere, as desired, or mix the two for a medium heat level.

2–3 SERVINGS

1 15-inch-long loaf Italian bread (about 1 pound)
⅓ cup bottled Italian dressing
3 tablespoons prepared pesto
½ cup pickled jardiniere vegetables
1 2¼-ounce can sliced ripe olives
8 ounces sliced Provolone cheese
1 7-ounce jar roasted red peppers
Romaine lettuce or spinach leaves

Cut bread in half lengthwise. Pull out soft bread crumbs, leaving a ½-inch-wide border, and reserve crumbs for another use. Combine dressing and pesto. Drain vegetables and olives well and add to dressing mixture. Spoon mixture evenly onto both sides of bread, then layer cheese evenly over both sides of bread. Rinse and drain peppers and dry between paper towels. Tear peppers into strips and place over cheese. Lay lettuce over peppers and close sandwich. Cut into serving size portions.

✤ *Serving suggestion:* Serve with potato salad.

CHEESY PESTO PINWHEELS

Cracker bread is available in gourmet markets and in the refrigerated section of some large supermarkets.

4 SERVINGS

1 15-inch-round thin cracker bread
6 ounces cream cheese, softened, or ⅔ cup
   soft cream cheese
3 tablespoons prepared pesto
1 large tomato
8 1-ounce slices Provolone, Monterey Jack,
   or Swiss cheese
3 large romaine lettuce leaves

Hold cracker bread briefly under cold running water to dampen one side. Place on a flat surface with dampened side down. Combine cream cheese and pesto and spread evenly over bread, leaving a ½-inch-wide border. Thinly slice tomato and shake out excess seeds and juice. Place tomato over cheese mixture. Arrange cheese slices in a single layer over tomato, leaving a 1-inch-wide border. Tear lettuce leaves in half and arrange over cheese. Roll up tightly and insert 4 wooden picks through roll to hold sandwich together while cutting. Cut crosswise into 4 pieces.

❧ *Serving suggestion:* Serve with navy bean soup.

QUICK CALZONES

In New York, calzones are sold by street vendors, catering to a lunchtime crowd that likes to eat on the run. You might prefer to enjoy this version sitting down, as the melted cheese and the sauce are deliciously suited to scooping up with a fork.

2 SERVINGS

1 10-ounce tube refrigerated pizza dough
⅓ cup prepared pizza sauce
1 cup preshredded mozzarella cheese
2 tablespoons prepared pesto
Olive oil or vegetable oil cooking spray

Heat oven to 450°F. Unroll pizza crust and cut in half crosswise. Spread pizza sauce evenly over both halves, leaving a ½-inch-wide border around the edges. Sprinkle cheese evenly over pizza sauce. Spoon pesto over cheese. Fold over half of dough to form a square pocket. Press edges firmly to seal. Spray a baking sheet with cooking spray. Transfer calzones to baking sheet and spray with cooking spray. Bake for about 12 minutes or until golden brown.

❧ *Serving suggestion:* Serve with a tossed green salad.

GRILLED EGGPLANT AND GOAT CHEESE SANDWICHES

Fresh goat cheese, sun-dried tomatoes, and meaty eggplant make this sandwich flavorful and quite filling.

2 SERVINGS

1 small (about 1 pound) eggplant
⅓ cup bottled vinaigrette salad dressing,
    divided
4 ounces goat cheese
4–6 bottled sun-dried tomato halves in
    oil, drained
Freshly ground black pepper
2 French bread baguettes
Basil or spinach leaves

Cut off and discard ends from eggplant. Cut lengthwise into ½-inch-thick slices. Brush both sides of slices with ¼ cup of the dressing. Grill or broil 5 inches from heat source for about 12 minutes or until tender, turning once. While eggplant is cooking, crumble cheese into a small bowl. Chop tomatoes and toss with cheese. Add pepper to taste.

Cut bread in half lengthwise. Brush both sides of bread with remaining dressing. Place cut-side down on grill or cut-side up under broiler alongside eggplant for about 1 minute, until lightly toasted. Place eggplant on bottom halves of bread and sprinkle with goat cheese mixture. Top with basil or spinach leaves; close sandwiches with tops of bread.

❧ *Serving suggestion:* Serve with Kalamata or Niçoise olives.

GREEK SALAD PITAS

Pitas are circle-shaped breads which, when cut in half, open up to form a "pocket" that's perfect for stuffing. They're perfect for ingredients, such as these, that would be a bit much to handle between two slices of bread.

4 SERVINGS

8 ounces feta cheese, crumbled
1 cup packed sliced romaine lettuce leaves
1 large tomato, seeded and chopped
½ cup thinly sliced unpeeled cucumber
  (slices halved if large)
¼ cup extra-virgin olive oil
2 tablespoons red wine vinegar or fresh
  lemon juice
½ teaspoon dried oregano leaves
¼ teaspoon salt
¼ teaspoon sugar
¼ teaspoon freshly ground black pepper
4 pita rounds, halved crosswise

Combine cheese, lettuce, tomato, and cucumber in a medium bowl. Combine oil, vinegar, oregano, salt, sugar, and pepper in another bowl and mix well. Toss with cheese mixture. Open pita pockets and fill with salad mixture.

❧ *Serving suggestion:* Serve with pepperoncini peppers.

Middle Eastern Hummos Pitas

Traditionally served as a dip for pita bread, hummos makes a hearty sandwich when vegetables are added. This version of hummos takes its flavor from Oriental sesame oil in place of tahini (a sesame seed paste), found in the Oriental section of large supermarkets.

2 SERVINGS

1 clove garlic
1 16-ounce can garbanzo beans
3 tablespoons extra-virgin olive oil
1½ tablespoons fresh lemon juice
1 teaspoon Oriental sesame oil
¼ teaspoon salt
2 pita rounds, halved crosswise
4 tomato slices
8 thin cucumber slices
¼ cup thinly sliced radishes

Peel garlic and place in a food processor fitted with the steel blade. Process until minced. Drain beans well, add to food processor, and process until beans are finely chopped. With the motor still running, add olive oil and lemon juice until mixture is almost smooth. Add sesame oil and salt and process until well blended. Open pita pockets and spread hummos evenly onto one side of each pocket. Add sliced tomato, cucumber, and radishes.

✄ *Serving suggestion:* Serve with tomato soup.

5
Soups, Stews, and Chili

Nothing is as comforting as a big bowl of steaming soup or stew on a chilly day. Luckily, it doesn't have to take all day to prepare—vegetable stews, for example, can be cooked to perfection in very little time.

You might want to try some of the many quality canned broths that are now readily available in grocery and specialty stores. They can help you create interesting, flavorful soups in almost no time at all.

Tomato, Spinach, and Basil Soup

Fresh basil is usually available all year long, but if it is unavailable, substitute 2 teaspoons dried basil. Leftover basil leaves may be minced in the food processor with garlic and enough olive oil to cover. Refrigerate up to 1 month. For a quick pesto sauce, add freshly grated aged Parmesan cheese.

4 SERVINGS (YIELD: 6 CUPS)

2 tablespoons butter or margarine
1 large yellow onion
1 teaspoon bottled minced garlic
1 teaspoon all-purpose flour
1½ cups milk
1 28-ounce can tomato puree
1 tablespoon sugar or to taste
2 cups prewashed spinach
Fresh basil leaves
½ teaspoon salt
¼ teaspoon freshly ground black pepper
Grated Parmesan cheese for garnish, if
   desired

Melt butter in a large saucepan over medium heat. Coarsely chop onion. Cook onion and garlic in butter for 3 minutes, stirring occasionally. Sprinkle onion with flour and cook for 30 seconds, stirring constantly. Stir in milk and cook for 2 minutes, stirring occasionally. Stir in tomato puree and sugar. Cover and bring to a boil over high heat. Stir soup, reduce heat to low, and simmer, covered, for 5 minutes.

While soup is cooking, tear spinach into bite-sized pieces and discard stems. Chop enough basil leaves to equal ¼ cup. Stir spinach, basil, salt, and pepper into soup and simmer, uncovered, for 2 minutes, stirring occasionally. Sprinkle with cheese, if desired.

🌿 *Serving suggestion:* Serve with grilled or toasted cheese sandwiches.

MINESTRONE

Minestrone is somewhat like Mom's homemade vegetable soup, but the tomatoes and herbs give it a rich, decidedly Italian flavor.

4 SERVINGS (YIELD: 6 CUPS)

2 14-ounce cans chicken broth (see note)
1 14½-ounce can stewed tomatoes,
    preferably chunky style
½ cup (about 2 ounces) small shell pasta,
    uncooked
1 teaspoon dried basil leaves
½ teaspoon marjoram or oregano leaves
¼ teaspoon freshly ground black pepper
2 medium carrots
1 8-ounce can kidney beans, drained
Chopped Italian or regular parsley, if
    desired
¼ cup grated Parmesan cheese

Combine broth, tomatoes, pasta, basil, marjoram, and pepper in a large saucepan. Cover and bring to a boil over high heat. Slice carrots thinly. Stir carrots and beans into soup and reduce heat to medium. Cover and simmer for 10 minutes or until carrots are tender. Sprinkle with parsley, if desired. Sprinkle with cheese.

❧ *Serving suggestion:* Serve with garlic croutons.

❧ *Note: Because the broth in this recipe greatly contributes to the flavor of the dish, vegetable broth (which does not have as much flavor) is not recommended. If, however, you prefer, you may use 3½ cups vegetable broth instead of chicken.*

HEARTY BEAN AND VEGETABLE SOUP

Cannellini beans are white kidney beans. If they are not located by the other canned beans, look for them in the Italian section of the supermarket.

4 SERVINGS (YIELD: 5½ CUPS)

1 14½-ounce can Italian-style stewed
    tomatoes, undrained
1 14-ounce can chicken broth (see note)
2 cups frozen mixed vegetable medley
    combination such as Italian green
    beans, broccoli, and red peppers
1 tablespoon chopped fresh basil or 1
    teaspoon dried basil
¼ teaspoon freshly ground black pepper
1 16- to 19-ounce can cannellini beans
¼ cup grated Parmesan cheese

Combine tomatoes, broth, frozen vegetables, basil, and pepper in a large saucepan. Cover and bring to a boil over high heat. Drain beans and stir into soup. Reduce heat to medium, cover, and simmer for 10 minutes. Sprinkle with cheese.

❧ *Serving suggestion:* Serve with Italian bread slices brushed with olive oil and garlic and lightly toasted.

❧ *Note: Because the broth in this recipe greatly contributes to the flavor of the dish, vegetable broth (which does not have as much flavor) is not recommended. If, however, you prefer, you may use 1¾ cups vegetable broth instead of chicken.*

BURGUNDY
MUSHROOM-VEGETABLE SOUP

Using your microwave oven to thaw frozen vegetables allows this hearty soup to be prepared and simmered in twenty minutes. If a microwave oven is not available, add frozen vegetables to soup and increase the simmer time by 6 minutes.

4 SERVINGS (YIELD: 4½ CUPS)

10 ounces (2½ cups) frozen mixed
    vegetables for stew (potatoes, carrots,
    onions, and celery)
2 tablespoons butter or margarine
3 cups (8 ounces) presliced mushrooms
1 teaspoon bottled minced garlic
1 tablespoon all-purpose flour
1 14-ounce can beef broth (see note)
¼ cup burgundy or other dry red wine
1 bay leaf
1 teaspoon dried thyme
½ teaspoon salt
¼ teaspoon freshly ground black pepper

Place frozen vegetables in a microwave-safe bowl. Microwave on defrost cycle (30% power) for 7 to 8 minutes.

While vegetables are defrosting, heat butter in a large saucepan over medium-high heat. Cook mushrooms and garlic in butter for 3 minutes, stirring occasionally. Add flour and cook for 1 minute, stirring constantly.

Add thawed vegetables, broth, wine, bay leaf, thyme, salt, and pepper. Bring to a boil over high heat. Reduce heat to low, cover, and simmer for 8 minutes, stirring occasionally. Remove and discard bay leaf.

✣ *Serving suggestion:* Serve with crusty hard rolls.

✣ *Note: Because the broth in this recipe greatly contributes to the flavor of the dish, vegetable broth (which does not have as much flavor) is not recommended. If, however, you prefer, you may use 1¾ cups vegetable broth instead of beef.*

HOT AND SOUR SOUP

Hot chili oil is found in the Oriental section of large super-markets by the Oriental sesame oil. If it is unavailable, substitute 1 teaspoon vegetable oil plus ½ teaspoon dried hot red pepper flakes.

4 SERVINGS (YIELD: 6 CUPS)

2 14-ounce cans chicken broth (see note)
2 tablespoons distilled vinegar
2 tablespoons soy sauce
1 teaspoon hot chili oil
¼ teaspoon ground white pepper
1 8- to 10-ounce package firm or extra
    firm tofu
½ 8-ounce can bamboo shoots, drained
1 15-ounce can or 2 7-ounce jars straw
    mushrooms, drained
2 green onions with tops
3 tablespoons water
2 tablespoons cornstarch
1 large egg white
1½ teaspoons Oriental sesame oil

Combine broth, vinegar, soy sauce, chili oil, and white pepper in a large saucepan. Cover and bring to a boil over high heat. Drain tofu, cut into ½-inch-thick cubes, and stir into soup. Reduce heat and simmer for 5 minutes. Cut bamboo shoots in half lengthwise. Stir bamboo shoots and mushrooms into soup. Continue to simmer for 5 minutes.

While soup is simmering, thinly slice green onions on the diagonal and set aside. Combine water and cornstarch, mixing until smooth, and stir into soup. Cook, uncovered, for 2 minutes or until thickened, stirring frequently. Beat egg white in a small bowl. Slowly pour egg white into soup in a thin stream while stirring constantly in one direction. Stir in reserved green onions and sesame oil.

❧ *Serving suggestion:* Serve with chow mein noodles.

❧ *Note: Because the broth in this recipe greatly contributes to the flavor of the dish, vegetable broth (which does not have as much flavor) is not recommended. If, however, you prefer, you may use 3½ cups vegetable broth instead of chicken.*

SWEET AND SOUR CABBAGE SOUP WITH PARMESAN TOAST

To quickly soften hard butter or margarine, place on a micro-wave-safe plate or paper plate and microwave at HIGH *power for 12 seconds or until softened.*

2–3 SERVINGS (YIELD: 4¹/₄ CUPS)

> 1 tablespoon olive or vegetable oil
> 1 large yellow onion
> 1 large yellow bell pepper
> 1 teaspoon bottled minced garlic
> 1 16-ounce jar sweet and sour cabbage,
>   undrained
> 1 14-ounce can beef broth (see note)
> 1 tablespoon packed brown sugar
> 4 large (about 6" X 3") oval slices
>   sourdough bread
> 2 tablespoons unsalted butter or
>   margarine, softened
> 3 tablespoons grated Parmesan cheese
> Sour cream for garnish

Heat oil in a medium saucepan over medium heat. Coarsely chop onion and place in saucepan. Coarsely chop bell pepper and add to saucepan. Add garlic and cook for 2 minutes, stirring occasionally. Add cabbage, broth, and sugar. Cover and bring to a boil over high heat. Reduce heat to low and simmer for 8 minutes, stirring occasionally.

While soup is simmering, heat broiler. Place bread on a baking sheet and broil 4 to 5 inches from heat source for 2 minutes or until lightly browned. Turn bread over, spread butter evenly over untoasted side of bread, and sprinkle with cheese. Return to broiler for 1 to 2 minutes or until golden brown.

Serve soup with Parmesan toast and sour cream.

❧ *Serving suggestion:* Serve with sliced avocado and tomato salad.

❧ *Note: Because the broth in this recipe greatly contributes to the flavor of the dish, vegetable broth (which does not have as much flavor) is not recommended. If, however, you prefer, you may use 1¾ cups vegetable broth instead of beef.*

ITALIAN ZUCCHINI SOUP

The addition of pizza sauce to a soup may seem a bit unconventional, but it gives a remarkable old-world flavor to the dish.

4 SERVINGS (YIELD: 5 CUPS)

1 14-ounce can chicken broth (see note)
1 14½-ounce can stewed tomatoes,
    preferably chunky style or Italian style,
    undrained
⅓ cup prepared pizza sauce
1 teaspoon dried basil
1 teaspoon dried oregano
¼ teaspoon dried hot red pepper flakes
1 large or 2 small zucchini and/or yellow
    squash (about 1 pound)
1 cup preshredded mozzarella cheese

Combine broth, tomatoes, pizza sauce, basil, oregano, and pepper flakes in a large saucepan. Cover and bring to a boil over high heat. Cut zucchini into ½-inch-thick pieces and stir into soup. Reduce heat to low, cover, and simmer for 8 to 10 minutes until squash is tender, stirring occasionally. Sprinkle with cheese.

✤ *Serving suggestion:* Serve with crusty Italian bread.

✤ *Note: Because the broth in this recipe greatly contributes to the flavor of the dish, vegetable broth (which does not have as much flavor) is not recommended. If, however, you prefer, you may use 1¾ cups vegetable broth instead of chicken.*

RAMEN NOODLE SOUP

Ramen noodles, which are very thin and curly, can be found in the Oriental section of the supermarket. Although they're often used as an accompaniment to Oriental dishes, this recipe features them as a tasty main ingredient.

2-3 SERVINGS (YIELD: 3³/₄ CUPS)

> 2 14-ounce cans chicken broth (see note)
> 1 3-ounce package ramen noodles with
>   dried vegetables
> 2 green onions with tops
> 2 teaspoons soy sauce
> ½ teaspoon hot chili oil
> ½ teaspoon bottled minced ginger
> 1 teaspoon Oriental sesame oil

Combine broth and noodles with dried vegetables in a medium saucepan. Cover and bring to a boil over high heat. Thinly slice green onions on the diagonal and set aside. Uncover soup and stir to break up noodles. Reduce heat to medium. Stir in soy sauce, chili oil, and ginger. Simmer, uncovered, for 10 minutes. Stir in sesame oil and sprinkle with green onions.

❧ *Serving suggestion:* Serve with melon wedges and fortune cookies.

❧ *Note: Because the broth in this recipe greatly contributes to the flavor of the dish, vegetable broth (which does not have as much flavor) is not recommended. If, however, you prefer, you may use 3½ cups vegetable broth instead of chicken.*

GREEK EGG-LEMON SOUP WITH PITA TOASTS

Orzo is a rice-shaped pasta that gives body to soups and stews.

2-3 SERVINGS (YIELD: 4 CUPS)

2 14-ounce cans chicken broth (see note)
⅓ cup orzo or quick-cooking brown rice,
    uncooked
2 pita rounds
1 tablespoon butter
1 tablespoon olive oil
½ teaspoon bottled minced garlic
½ teaspoon dried oregano
2 large eggs
2 tablespoons fresh lemon juice
Chopped parsley for garnish, if desired

Heat oven to 375°F. Combine broth and orzo in a medium saucepan. Cover and bring to a boil over high heat. Reduce heat to low, cover, and simmer for 10 to 12 minutes or until orzo is tender.

While orzo is cooking, cut pita rounds into 6 wedges each. Open each wedge and break into 2 triangles. Place rough-side up on a large baking sheet. Place butter in a small microwave-safe cup or bowl and microwave at HIGH power for 1 minute or until melted. Stir in oil, garlic, and oregano and brush evenly over pita triangles. Bake for 9 to 10 minutes or until crisp and golden brown.

While pita is baking, beat eggs in a small bowl. Beat in lemon juice. After soup has simmered and orzo is tender, stir 1 cup soup slowly into egg mixture, mixing constantly. Remove soup from heat. Pour egg mixture slowly into soup while stirring constantly. Sprinkle with parsley, if desired, and serve with pita toasts.

❧ *Serving suggestion:* Serve with a tossed salad of romaine lettuce, sliced cucumbers, Greek olives, and red wine vinaigrette dressing.

❧ *Note: Because the broth in this recipe greatly contributes to the flavor of the dish, vegetable broth (which does not have as much flavor) is not recommended. If, however, you prefer, you may use 3½ cups vegetable broth instead of chicken.*

SPICY BLACK BEAN SOUP
WITH NACHOS

Salsa verde is a spicy green tomatillo sauce found in the ethnic section of large supermarkets. If it is unavailable, substitute prepared hot salsa or picante sauce.

4 SERVINGS (YIELD: 4 CUPS)

1 tablespoon vegetable oil
1 medium yellow onion
1 teaspoon bottled minced garlic
1 14-ounce can beef or chicken broth (see note)
1 16-ounce can black beans, undrained
⅓ cup salsa verde
1 teaspoon ground cumin
¼ teaspoon salt
3 ounces yellow, white, or blue corn tortilla chips
1 cup preshredded Cojack or cheddar cheese
Sliced pickled jalapeño peppers, if desired
Sour cream for garnish
Chopped cilantro for garnish
Prepared salsa or picante sauce for garnish

Heat oven to 375°F. Heat oil in a medium saucepan over medium heat. Coarsely chop onion. Cook onion and garlic in oil for 2 minutes, stirring occasionally. Add broth, beans, salsa verde, cumin, and salt. Cover and bring to a boil over high heat. Stir soup and reduce heat to low. Cover and simmer for 8 minutes.

While soup is simmering, spread chips on a foil-lined baking sheet in one layer. Sprinkle evenly with cheese and jalapeño peppers, if desired. Bake for 7 to 8 minutes or until chips are heated and cheese is melted and bubbly.

While chips are baking, process soup in two batches in a food processor fitted with the steel blade until almost smooth. Serve soup with sour cream and cilantro accompanied by nachos and salsa.

❧ *Serving suggestion:* Serve with a Caesar salad.

❧ *Note: Because the broth in this recipe greatly contributes to the flavor of the dish, vegetable broth (which does not have as much flavor) is not recommended. If, however, you prefer, you may use 1¾ cups vegetable broth instead of chicken or beef.*

TORTILLA SOUP

Although it's served hot, this south-of-the-border treat is perfect for summer nights as well as chillier evenings.

2 – 3 SERVINGS (YIELD: 4 CUPS)

1 14-ounce can chicken broth (see note)
1 14½-ounce can Mexican stewed
   tomatoes, undrained
½ cup prepared salsa or picante sauce
1 teaspoon ground cumin
4 7- to 8-inch corn tortillas
1 cup preshredded Monterey Jack cheese
½ cup thinly sliced green onion
¼ cup coarsely chopped cilantro

Combine broth, tomatoes, salsa, and cumin in a medium saucepan. Cover and bring to a boil over high heat. Reduce heat to low and simmer for 10 minutes, stirring occasionally. While soup is cooking, cut tortillas into 1-inch-wide squares and place in soup bowls. Place cheese over tortillas in soup bowls. After soup has simmered for 10 minutes, stir in green onion and cilantro. Ladle soup into soup bowls over cheese and tortillas.

❧ *Serving suggestion:* Serve with lime wedges and a crisp vegetable salad with a lime vinaigrette dressing.

❧ *Note: Because the broth in this recipe greatly contributes to the flavor of the dish, vegetable broth (which does not have as much flavor) is not recommended. If, however, you prefer, you may use 1¾ cups vegetable broth instead of chicken.*

CURRIED RICE SOUP

Unsweetened coconut milk may be found in the ethnic or Thai section of large supermarkets or in specialty food stores. If you are using Madras (hot) curry powder, omit the cayenne pepper.

4 SERVINGS (YIELD: 4½ CUPS)

1 tablespoon vegetable oil
1 small yellow onion
2 teaspoons curry powder
1 teaspoon bottled minced ginger
¼ teaspoon cayenne pepper
1 14-ounce can unsweetened coconut milk
1 14-ounce can chicken broth (see note)
¾ cup quick-cooking brown rice
½ teaspoon salt
1 tablespoon fresh lime juice
Chopped cilantro for garnish, if desired

Heat oil in a large saucepan over medium heat. Coarsely chop onion, add to oil, and cook for 2 minutes. Add curry powder, ginger, and cayenne pepper and cook for 1 minute, stirring frequently. Add coconut milk, broth, rice, and salt. Cover and bring to a boil over high heat. Reduce heat to low and stir soup. Cover and simmer for 8 to 10 minutes or until rice is tender. Stir in lime juice and sprinkle with cilantro, if desired.

❧ *Serving suggestion:* Serve with sliced ripe papaya.

❧ *Note: If desired, substitute 1¾ cups vegetable broth or 1¾ cups water plus ¼ teaspoon salt for chicken broth.*

SHERRIED MUSHROOM SOUP

A hint of sherry makes this creamy soup rather sophisticated. For a more exotic mushroom soup, substitute halved fresh oyster mushrooms or sliced fresh shiitake mushroom caps for half the regular mushrooms. (Note: cleaning and slicing will add an additional 5 minutes to the time required to prepare this dish.)

4 SERVINGS (YIELD: 5 CUPS)

¼ cup butter or margarine

1 small yellow onion

3 cups (9 ounces) presliced mushrooms

½ teaspoon bottled minced garlic

¼ cup all-purpose flour

¼ teaspoon rubbed sage, if desired

2 10¾-ounce cans condensed chicken
    broth (see note)

1 cup milk

1 tablespoon Worcestershire sauce

¼ teaspoon freshly ground black pepper

2 tablespoons dry sherry

Chopped parsley, if desired

Melt butter in a large saucepan over medium heat. Coarsely chop onion. Cook onion, mushrooms, and garlic in butter for 3 minutes, stirring occasionally. Add flour and sage, if desired, and cook for 1 minute, stirring constantly. Stir in broth, milk,

Worcestershire sauce, and pepper. Cover and bring to a boil over high heat. Stir soup and reduce heat to low. Cover and simmer for 6 to 8 minutes. Remove from heat and stir in sherry. Sprinkle with parsley, if desired.

❧ *Serving suggestion:* Serve with soft bread sticks.

❧ *Note: Because the broth in this recipe greatly contributes to the flavor of the dish, vegetable broth (which does not have as much flavor) is not recommended. If, however, you prefer, you may use 2 6-ounce jars condensed vegetable broth (available in some specialty food stores) plus 1 cup water instead of chicken.*

SWEET POTATO CHOWDER

This is a southern favorite that uses the sweet potato to its most flavorful advantage.

4 SERVINGS (YIELD: 4½ CUPS)

2 tablespoons butter or margarine
1 small yellow onion
¼ teaspoon cayenne pepper
1 16-ounce can cut sweet potatoes or
  yams, drained
1 14-ounce can chicken broth, divided (see
  note)
1 8-ounce can whole kernel corn, drained
½ cup half-and-half or milk
¼ teaspoon salt
Prepared croutons for garnish, if desired

Melt butter in a medium saucepan over medium heat. Coarsely chop onion. Cook onion and cayenne pepper in butter for 3 minutes, stirring occasionally. Add sweet potatoes and 1 cup of the broth. Cover and bring to a boil over high heat. Reduce heat to low and simmer for 5 minutes or until potatoes are very tender.

Transfer mixture to a food processor fitted with the steel blade. Process until fairly smooth. Return to saucepan. Add remaining broth, corn, half-and-half, and salt. Cook, uncovered, for 1 to 2 minutes or until heated through, stirring constantly. Sprinkle with croutons, if desired.

❧ *Serving suggestion:* Serve with a salad of mixed bitter greens with a vinaigrette dressing.

❧ Note: *Because the broth in this recipe greatly contributes to the flavor of the dish, vegetable broth (which does not have as much flavor) is not recommended. If, however, you prefer, you may use 1¾ cups vegetable broth instead of chicken.*

CREAMY CORN AND POTATO CHOWDER

For a richer chowder, substitute half-and-half for the milk. There is no need to thaw the potatoes before cooking.

2–3 SERVINGS (YIELD: 4 CUPS)

1½ cups milk
1 17-ounce can cream-style corn
2 cups (8 ounces) frozen ready-to-cook
    hash brown potatoes with peppers and
    onions (O'Brien style)
1 teaspoon salt
¼ teaspoon freshly ground black pepper
½ cup preshredded sharp cheddar cheese
Chopped chives or green onion tops for
    garnish, if desired

Combine milk, corn, potatoes, salt, and pepper in a large saucepan. Cover and bring to a boil over high heat. Reduce heat to medium-low. Uncover and stir to break up potatoes. Simmer, uncovered, for 8 to 10 minutes or until thickened, stirring frequently. Sprinkle with cheese and chives, if desired.

✤ *Serving suggestion:* Serve with oyster crackers and carrot and celery sticks.

JAMBALAYA

This Louisiana-inspired stew is rich and fairly thick. For a thinner stew, add additional broth. (It's a good idea to keep cubes of chicken, beef, and vegetable bouillon in the pantry to make quick broths for any soup or stew.)

4 SERVINGS (YIELD: 6 CUPS)

1 28-ounce can Italian plum tomatoes, undrained
1 cup chicken, beef, or vegetable broth
1 cup quick-cooking brown rice
1 teaspoon bottled minced garlic
2 bay leaves
1 teaspoon dried basil leaves
1 teaspoon dried thyme leaves
¾–1 teaspoon hot pepper sauce, as desired
1 large green bell pepper
1 16-ounce can black-eyed peas, drained
Chopped parsley or chives for garnish, if desired

Combine tomatoes, broth, rice, garlic, bay leaves, basil, thyme, and hot pepper sauce in a large saucepan. Cover and bring to a boil over high heat.

While rice is cooking, cut green pepper into 1-inch pieces and stir into stew. Reduce heat to medium. Stir in black-eyed peas, cover, and simmer for 10 to 12 minutes, stirring once. Remove and discard bay leaves. Sprinkle with parsley, if desired.

❧ *Serving suggestion:* Serve with garlic bread.

RATATOUILLE STEW

Two large zucchini squash may be substituted for one zucchini and one yellow squash.

5-6 SERVINGS (YIELD: 8 CUPS)

- 2 14½-ounce cans stewed tomatoes, undrained
- 1 14-ounce can chicken or beef broth (see note)
- 1 small (about 1 pound) eggplant
- 1 large (about 8 ounces) zucchini squash
- 1 large (about 8 ounces) yellow squash
- 1½ teaspoons bottled minced garlic
- 1 teaspoon sugar
- 1 teaspoon dried basil
- 1 teaspoon dried thyme
- ¼ teaspoon dried hot red pepper flakes
- 1½ cups preshredded mozzarella cheese

Combine tomatoes and broth in a large saucepan. Cover and bring to a boil over high heat. Cut eggplant crosswise into ¾-inch-wide slices. Cut slices into ¾-inch-thick cubes. Stir into saucepan and cover. Cut zucchini and yellow squash into ½-inch-wide slices. Cut each slice in quarters. Stir into saucepan with garlic, sugar, basil, thyme, and pepper flakes and reduce heat to low. Cover and simmer for 8 minutes, stirring occasionally. Sprinkle with cheese.

❧ *Serving suggestion:* Serve with crusty Italian bread or hard rolls.

❧ Note: *Because the broth in this recipe greatly contributes to the flavor of the dish, vegetable broth (which does not have as much flavor) is not recommended. If, however, you prefer, you may use 1¾ cups vegetable broth instead of chicken or beef.*

OLD WORLD GOULASH

Look for tins of Hungarian paprika in the spice section of your supermarket. Both sweet and hot paprika are available in most large supermarkets.

4 SERVINGS (YIELD: 5 CUPS)

1 tablespoon olive or vegetable oil
1 large yellow onion
1 teaspoon bottled minced garlic
2 teaspoons sweet Hungarian paprika
¼ teaspoon hot Hungarian paprika or
    cayenne pepper
1 14-ounce can chicken broth (see note)
1 14½-ounce can stewed tomatoes,
    preferably chunky style
1 8-ounce can whole kernel corn,
    undrained
1 teaspoon dried marjoram or basil
1½ cups (3 ounces) thin egg noodles,
    uncooked
Sour cream for garnish

Heat oil in a large saucepan over medium-high heat. Coarsely chop onion. Cook onion and garlic in oil for 3 minutes, stirring occasionally. Add sweet and hot paprika and cook for 30 seconds, stirring constantly. Stir in broth, tomatoes, corn, and marjoram. Cover and bring to a boil over high heat. Reduce heat to medium-low and stir noodles into soup. Cover and simmer for 6 to 7 minutes or until noodles are tender. Serve with sour cream.

✻ *Serving suggestion:* Serve with assorted crackers.

✻ Note: *Because the broth in this recipe greatly contributes to the flavor of the dish, vegetable broth (which does not have as much flavor) is not recommended. If, however, you prefer, you may use 1¾ cups vegetable broth instead of chicken.*

TORTELLINI AND SPINACH STEW

If prewashed packaged spinach is not available in your produce section, purchase torn spinach, escarole, or romaine leaves from the salad bar.

2 SERVINGS (YIELD: 4 CUPS)

1 9-ounce package refrigerated cheese-
   filled tortellini, uncooked
2 cups packed prewashed spinach leaves
2 medium tomatoes or 4 plum tomatoes
2 tablespoons olive oil
2 teaspoons bottled minced garlic
1 cup chicken, beef, or vegetable broth
2 tablespoons minced fresh basil or 1
   teaspoon dried basil
⅓ cup grated Asiago or Parmesan cheese
Freshly ground black pepper for garnish

Cook tortellini according to package directions. While tortellini is cooking, remove stems from spinach leaves and set aside. Seed and chop tomatoes and set aside. Heat oil in a large deep skillet over medium-high heat. Add garlic and cook for 1 minute. Add broth and boil gently, uncovered, for 5 minutes. Add spinach, tomato, and basil and heat through just until spinach wilts. Drain tortellini and add to skillet. Cook for 1 minute or until hot. Sprinkle with cheese and serve with pepper.

❧ *Serving suggestion:* Serve with crisp bread sticks.

THREE-BEAN CHILI

Nothing beats chili for a satisfying, hearty meal—especially if it can be prepared in under twenty minutes. For a richer, darker chili, stir in 1 teaspoon unsweetened cocoa along with the chili powder.

4 SERVINGS (YIELD: 6 CUPS)

1 16-ounce can chili beans in spicy broth,
    undrained
1 16-ounce can black beans, drained
1 16-ounce can pinto or red kidney beans,
    drained
1 14½-ounce can Mexican-style stewed
    tomatoes, undrained
¾ cup beef, chicken, or vegetable broth
1 tablespoon ground cumin
1 tablespoon chili powder
1 large red or green bell pepper

Combine chili beans, black beans, pinto beans, tomatoes, broth, cumin, and chili powder in a large saucepan. Cover and bring to a boil over high heat. While beans are cooking, chop bell pepper and stir into chili. Reduce heat to medium, cover, and continue cooking for 10 minutes, stirring occasionally.

❧ *Serving suggestion:* Serve with corn bread or corn muffins and toppings for chili such as sour cream, preshredded cheddar cheese, chopped cilantro, diced avocado, and prepared salsa or picante sauce.

6
Pasta

❧

Both the Italians and the Chinese have long been lovers of meatless pasta and noodle dishes. These dishes are now widely acclaimed by athletes, who have found that the rich complex carbohydrates in pastas provide bountiful energy needed for competitions and endurance training. As an added bonus, pastas are extremely low in fat as well.

Take advantage of the abundance of dried and fresh pastas that are now readily available in supermarkets—they're a flavorful alternative to the standard spaghetti noodles most of us grew up with.

To cook pasta, follow the directions on the package, and taste it toward the end of cooking. Pasta should be tender, but still firm to the bite. Note that fresh pastas cook more quickly than dried, so be careful to avoid overcooking them.

MOSTACCIOLI WITH GARDEN-FRESH TOMATO SAUCE

This dish is best when homegrown or vine-ripened tomatoes are used. When they aren't available, substitute hydroponically grown or hothouse tomatoes.

Olive paste (ground salted olives in olive oil) may be found in specialty food stores or in the Italian section of large supermarkets. If unavailable, substitute ¼ cup chopped Niçoise or Kalamata olives.

4 SERVINGS

8 ounces mostaccioli or ziti pasta,
   uncooked
½ cup extra-virgin olive oil
⅓ cup packed fresh basil leaves
1 tablespoon prepared bottled olive paste
1 tablespoon balsamic vinegar
2 teaspoons bottled minced garlic
¾ teaspoon salt
½ teaspoon freshly ground black pepper
¼ teaspoon dried hot red pepper flakes
2 pounds ripe tomatoes
½ cup grated Parmesan cheese

Cook pasta according to package directions. While pasta is cooking, place oil in a large serving bowl. Chop basil and add to oil. Stir in olive paste. Stir in vinegar, garlic, salt, pepper, and pepper flakes.

Place a strainer over the bowl. Cut tomatoes in half and squeeze juices into strainer. Discard seeds. Coarsely chop tomatoes, add to bowl, and toss well.

Drain pasta and add to bowl. Toss well and sprinkle with cheese.

❧ *Serving suggestion:* Serve with warm crusty Italian bread and extra-virgin olive oil for dipping.

CAPELLINI PUTTANESCA

Look for resealable tubes of tomato paste in the Italian or imported foods section of your supermarket.

4 SERVINGS

8 ounces capellini or angel hair pasta,
  uncooked
2 tablespoons olive oil
2 teaspoons bottled minced garlic
½ teaspoon dried hot red pepper flakes
1 16-ounce can plum tomatoes, undrained
2 tablespoons tomato paste
1½ tablespoons drained capers
½ cup drained Kalamata olives
¼ cup chopped fresh Italian parsley,
  regular parsley, or basil leaves for
  garnish, if desired
¼ cup grated Parmesan cheese

Cook pasta according to package directions. While pasta is cooking, heat oil in a large deep skillet or saucepan over medium-high heat. Add garlic and pepper flakes and cook for 1 minute. Add tomatoes, breaking up with a wooden spoon. Stir in tomato paste and capers, cover, and bring to a boil. Reduce heat and simmer for 6 minutes.

While tomatoes are cooking, remove and discard olive pits and cut olives in half. Stir into sauce. Drain pasta and toss with sauce. Sprinkle with parsley, if desired, and cheese.

❧ *Serving suggestion:* Serve with fresh fruit and wedges of Camembert or Brie cheese.

ITALIAN PASTA PIPERADE

Piperade is a combination of sautéed strips of sweet peppers common to Italian cuisine.

4 SERVINGS

12 ounces capellini or thin spaghetti,
   uncooked
3 small bell peppers, preferably one red,
   one yellow or orange, and one green
1 tablespoon olive oil
1 teaspoon bottled minced garlic
1 28-ounce jar prepared spaghetti sauce
¼ cup packed fresh basil leaves
¼ cup grated Parmesan or Romano cheese

Cook pasta according to package directions. While pasta is cooking, cut bell peppers lengthwise into thin strips. Heat oil in a large skillet over medium heat. Add pepper strips and garlic, cover, and cook for 6 to 7 minutes or until tender, stirring occasionally. Add spaghetti sauce. Simmer, uncovered, for 3 minutes until heated through.

   Cut basil leaves into thin strips. Drain pasta and add pasta and basil to sauce. Toss well. Sprinkle with cheese.

❧ *Serving suggestion:* Serve with a fruit salad.

ZITI WITH TOMATO SAUCE AND MOZZARELLA

Fresh mozzarella cheese, which is packaged in brine, has a creamier texture than regular mozzarella cheese. It may be found in specialty food shops, Italian markets, or some large supermarkets. If it is unavailable, substitute regular mozzarella cheese.

If fresh basil is not available, add 2 teaspoons dried basil to the tomato sauce.

4 SERVINGS

12 ounces ziti, penne, or bowtie pasta,
    uncooked
2 tablespoons olive oil
1 small yellow onion
1 teaspoon bottled minced garlic
1 28-ounce can crushed tomatoes in
    tomato puree
1 teaspoon sugar
¾ teaspoon salt
¼ teaspoon dried hot red pepper flakes
¼ cup packed fresh basil leaves
8 ounces fresh mozzarella cheese
2 tablespoons balsamic vinegar
Grated Parmesan cheese for garnish

Cook pasta according to package directions. While pasta is cooking, heat oil in a large saucepan over medium heat. Coarsely chop onion, add onion and garlic to oil, and cook for 2 minutes. Add tomatoes, sugar, salt, and pepper flakes and bring to a boil. Reduce heat and simmer, uncovered, for 5 minutes.

While tomatoes are cooking, cut basil leaves into thin strips. Cut cheese into ¾-inch-thick pieces and set aside.

Drain pasta, add to tomato sauce, and toss lightly. Add vinegar, basil, and cheese and toss again. Serve with Parmesan cheese.

❧ *Serving suggestion:* Serve with a mixed salad of bitter greens tossed with Italian dressing.

PASTA PRIMAVERA

Presliced packaged mushrooms are available in the produce section of large supermarkets. If they are unavailable, purchase sliced mushrooms from the salad bar.

4 SERVINGS

> 8 ounces ziti, medium shell, or bowtie
> pasta, uncooked
> ¾ pound fresh asparagus or 1 pound
> broccoli
> 1 cup frozen baby peas
> 3 tablespoons butter or margarine
> 2 cups (6 ounces) presliced mushrooms
> 1 teaspoon bottled minced garlic
> ⅓ cup half-and-half
> ¼ teaspoon dried hot red pepper flakes
> ¼ teaspoon salt
> ½ cup grated Asiago or Romano cheese
> Freshly ground black pepper for garnish
> Lemon wedges for garnish, if desired

Cook pasta according to package directions. Trim asparagus, cut into ¾-inch-long pieces (or cut broccoli into large florets and save stalks for another use), and add to pasta water during last 3 minutes of cooking. Add peas to pasta water during last 1 minute of cooking.

While the pasta and vegetables are cooking, melt butter in a large deep skillet over medium-high heat. Add mushrooms and garlic and cook 3 minutes, stirring occasionally. Add half-and-half, pepper flakes, and salt and heat through.

Drain pasta and vegetables well. Add to skillet and toss well. Toss with cheese, sprinkle with pepper to taste, and serve with lemon wedges, if desired.

꙳ *Serving suggestion:* Serve with garlic bread.

PASTA WITH VEGETABLES IN PEPPER CHEESE SAUCE

Use your favorite vegetable combination in this light, flavorful dish.

4 SERVINGS

8 ounces bowtie, medium shells, or
    mostaccioli pasta, uncooked
8 ounces frozen mixed vegetable medley
    (any variety)
3 ounces cream cheese, softened
1 6½- or 7-ounce jar roasted red peppers
6 large basil leaves or ½ teaspoon dried
    basil
½ teaspoon freshly ground black pepper
¼ teaspoon salt
Grated Parmesan cheese for garnish, if
    desired.

Cook pasta according to package directions. Add frozen vegetables to the water during last 5 minutes of pasta cooking time. While pasta is cooking, place cream cheese in a food processor fitted with the steel blade. Process until smooth.

Drain, rinse, and pat roasted peppers dry with paper towel. Add to food processor with basil, pepper, and salt. Process until smooth, scraping down sides once. Transfer sauce to a large bowl. Drain pasta and vegetables, add to bowl, and toss well. Sprinkle with cheese, if desired.

❧ *Serving suggestion:* Serve with a Caesar salad.

CREAMY GARLIC FETTUCCINE

Parmesano Reggiano cheese is an Italian aged Parmesan cheese available in large supermarkets or specialty food stores. It is best when grated just before it is used.

4 SERVINGS

8 ounces fettuccine, uncooked
3 ounces Parmesan cheese, preferably
   Parmesano Reggiano
¼ cup butter or margarine
2 cloves fresh garlic
1 cup half-and-half
½ teaspoon salt
Freshly ground black pepper for garnish

Cook pasta according to package directions. While pasta is cooking, finely grate cheese and set aside. Melt butter in a 10-inch skillet over medium-high heat. Peel garlic and force through a garlic press or mince. Add garlic to skillet and cook for 1 minute. Add half-and-half and salt and simmer, uncovered, for 5 minutes or until thickened, stirring occasionally.

Drain pasta and add to skillet. Add cheese and cook over low heat for about 2 minutes, until sauce thickens, tossing constantly with 2 wooden spoons. Serve with pepper.

❧ *Serving suggestion:* Serve with crusty Italian hard rolls.

MACARONI WITH WHITE CHEDDAR SAUCE

White cheddar cheese may be found in specialty or gourmet markets and deli counters. If it is unavailable, substitute aged sharp cheddar cheese.

4 SERVINGS

8 ounces large elbow macaroni, uncooked
6 ounces sharp white cheddar cheese
3 tablespoons butter or margarine
¾ cup whipping cream
½ teaspoon salt
¼ teaspoon ground white pepper
Chopped parsley or chives for garnish, if
   desired

Cook macaroni according to package directions. While macaroni is cooking, shred cheese and set aside. Melt butter in a 10-inch skillet over medium heat. Add cream, salt, and pepper and bring to a boil.

Drain macaroni and add to skillet. Cook for 1 to 2 minutes or until macaroni is coated evenly with sauce, stirring occasionally. Add cheese to skillet and stir until cheese is melted. Sprinkle with parsley, if desired.

❧ *Serving suggestion:* Serve with pumpernickel bread.

LINGUINE WITH GORGONZOLA SAUCE

Gorgonzola is Italy's answer to bleu cheese—it has a similar appearance, but melts more easily. It also has a bit more of a bite than its French cousin.

4 SERVINGS

1 9-ounce package refrigerated linguine or
  spinach linguine, uncooked
½ cup pine nuts
6 ounces Gorgonzola or Stilton cheese
1 cup whipping cream
Freshly ground black pepper for garnish
¼ cup thinly sliced fresh basil leaves for
  garnish, if desired

Cook linguine according to package directions. While linguine is cooking, toast pine nuts in a toaster oven or conventional oven at 350°F for 5 to 7 minutes or until deep golden brown. Crumble cheese into a large saucepan, add cream, and cook over medium heat for 5 minutes or until cheese is melted and sauce is simmering, stirring frequently.

Drain linguine, add to saucepan, and toss with sauce. Cook for 1 minute or until sauce has thickened and linguine is coated. Stir in pine nuts. Serve with pepper and sprinkle with basil leaves, if desired.

❧ *Serving suggestion:* Serve with a spinach salad tossed with red onion rings, olives, and Italian dressing.

MUSHROOM STROGANOFF

This is a rich, creamy meat-free version of the classic beef stroganoff. Served with your favorite red wine, it makes for an easy yet elegant meal.

4 SERVINGS

8 ounces egg noodles, uncooked
2 tablespoons butter or margarine
1 medium yellow onion
1 teaspoon bottled minced garlic
4 cups (12 ounces) presliced mushrooms
2 tablespoons brandy or cognac, if desired
1 tablespoon Worcestershire sauce
1 tablespoon Dijon-style mustard
1 cup sour cream
2 teaspoons all-purpose flour
Fresh chopped chives for garnish, if
    desired
Freshly ground black pepper for garnish

Cook noodles according to package directions. While noodles are cooking, melt butter in a large skillet over medium heat. Coarsely chop onion. Place onion and garlic in skillet and cook for 2 minutes, stirring occasionally. Add mushrooms and cook for 4 minutes, stirring occasionally. Add brandy, if desired, and carefully ignite with a lighted match. Shake skillet until flames subside. Add Worcestershire sauce and mustard and mix well.

Combine sour cream and flour in a small bowl and mix well. Reduce heat to medium-low and stir sour cream mixture into mushroom mixture. Cook for 2 to 3 minutes or until thickened and bubbly, stirring frequently.

Drain noodles well and spoon mushroom mixture over noodles. Sprinkle with chives, if desired. Serve with pepper.

🌱 *Serving suggestion:* Serve with rye or pumpernickel rolls or bread.

SZECHUAN NOODLES

Look for bottled minced ginger in the produce section of the supermarket. If it is unavailable, shred fresh gingerroot on the small side of a cheese grater. Keep fresh gingerroot in a freezer bag in the freezer up to 6 months. There is no need to defrost or peel the gingerroot before shredding.

4 SERVINGS

8 ounces Chinese egg noodles or
    vermicelli, uncooked
8 ounces shiitake, crimini, or button
    mushrooms
8 ounces snow pea pods
4 tablespoons peanut or vegetable oil,
    divided
1 teaspoon bottled minced garlic
1 teaspoon bottled minced ginger
½ teaspoon dried hot red pepper flakes
3 tablespoons soy sauce
2 tablespoons rice vinegar or seasoned rice
    vinegar
1 tablespoon Oriental sesame oil
¼ cup roasted salted peanuts for garnish,
    if desired

Cook noodles according to package directions. While noodles are cooking, discard stems from shiitake mushrooms and slice caps. (If other mushrooms are used, slice them with stems intact.) Trim ends and cut pea pods lengthwise in half and set aside.

Heat 2 tablespoons of the oil in a large skillet or wok over medium-high heat until hot. Add mushrooms, garlic, ginger, and pepper flakes. Stir-fry for 2 minutes. Add pea pods and stir-fry for 2 minutes.

Combine soy sauce, vinegar, and sesame oil in a small bowl. Drain noodles and add to skillet. Add soy sauce mixture to skillet. Toss well and heat through. Sprinkle with peanuts, if desired.

❧ *Serving suggestion:* Serve with a chilled cucumber salad.

Vegetable Lo Mein

Oriental sesame oil, oyster sauce, and lo mein noodles may be found in the ethnic section of large supermarkets. Bok choy is a Chinese vegetable widely available in large supermarkets.

4 SERVINGS

8 ounces lo mein noodles, uncooked
4 large stalks bok choy
1 tablespoon peanut or vegetable oil
2 cups (6 ounces) presliced mushrooms
1 teaspoon bottled minced garlic
1 teaspoon bottled minced ginger
1 6-ounce package frozen snow pea pods
½ cup vegetable or chicken broth
3 tablespoons soy sauce
2 tablespoons oyster sauce
2 tablespoons Oriental sesame oil
Coarsely chopped cashews for garnish

Cook noodles according to package directions. While noodles are cooking, cut bok choy into ½-inch slices. Heat peanut oil in a large deep skillet or wok over medium-high heat until hot. Add bok choy, mushrooms, garlic, and ginger and stir-fry for 2 minutes. Add pea pods and stir-fry for 2 minutes.

Combine broth, soy sauce, and oyster sauce in a small bowl and add to skillet. Drain noodles well and add to skillet. Cook for 2 minutes or until heated through, stirring occassionally. Stir in sesame oil and sprinkle with cashews.

Serving suggestion: Serve with cantaloupe or honeydew melon wedges.

Tex-Mex Spaghetti

Picante sauce gives this spaghetti a rich southwestern flavor.

3–4 SERVINGS

8 ounces spaghetti or spaghettini,
  uncooked
1 tablespoon vegetable oil
1 small yellow onion
1 teaspoon bottled minced garlic
1 14½-ounce can Mexican-style or regular
  stewed tomatoes, undrained
1 cup mild picante sauce
1 teaspoon ground cumin
½ teaspoon dried oregano leaves
1 16-ounce can pinto beans
1 cup preshredded Cojack or cheddar
  cheese

Cook pasta according to package directions. While pasta is cooking, heat oil in a 10-inch skillet over medium heat. Coarsely chop onion and place in skillet. Add garlic and cook for 2 minutes, stirring occasionally. Add tomatoes, picante sauce, cumin, and oregano. Cover and bring to a boil over high heat. Reduce heat, uncover, and simmer for 5 minutes, stirring occasionally.

Drain beans and stir into tomato mixture. Continue to simmer, uncovered, for 5 minutes or until thickened, stirring frequently. Drain pasta and top with sauce and cheese.

❧ *Serving suggestion:* Serve with warm flour or corn tortillas.

7
Pizza

Pizza is perhaps the most popular dish ever to come from Italy. Over the years, it's come a long way from the simple cheese-and-sauce combinations that established it as a favorite in American cuisine. Happily, pizza continues to be one of the most flexible meals around—well suited to meat-free ingredients all year round. In addition, the introduction of ready-made pizza crusts in grocery stores makes this entree amazingly quick and easy to prepare.

PIZZA MARGARITA

Baking the pizza directly on the oven rack produces a crisper crust in less baking time. To aid in oven cleanup, place a sheet of heavy-duty aluminum foil on the bottom oven rack to catch any drips from pizza.

4 SERVINGS

½ *cup prepared pizza sauce*
1 *12-inch prepared pizza crust*
¼ *teaspoon dried hot red pepper flakes*
2 *cups preshredded mozzarella cheese*
2 *medium tomatoes or 4 plum tomatoes*
3 *tablespoons refrigerated pesto sauce*
3 *tablespoons grated Parmesan cheese*

Heat oven to 450°F. Spread pizza sauce evenly over crust and sprinkle with pepper flakes. Sprinkle mozzarella evenly over sauce. Slice tomatoes very thinly, shake out excess juices and seeds, and place over cheese. Spread pesto over tomatoes and sprinkle Parmesan cheese evenly over all. Bake directly on oven rack for 9 to 10 minutes or until cheese is melted. Slide a cookie sheet under the hot pizza to remove from oven. Cut into wedges.

❧ *Serving suggestion:* Serve with a marinated vegetable salad.

MUSHROOM AND
GOAT CHEESE PIZZA

If fresh shiitake mushrooms are not available, substitute sliced fresh button or crimini (brown) mushrooms.

2 SERVINGS

8 ounces fresh shiitake mushrooms
3 tablespoons olive oil, preferably extra-
   virgin, divided
1 teaspoon bottled minced garlic
¼ teaspoon dried rosemary, crushed
¼ teaspoon dried thyme
2 6-inch prepared pizza crusts
4 ounces goat cheese or herbed goat cheese
Freshly ground black pepper to taste

Heat oven to 450°F. Wipe mushrooms with a damp paper towel. Discard stems and slice caps. Heat 2 tablespoons oil in a 10-inch skillet over medium-high heat. Add mushrooms, garlic, rosemary, and thyme. Cook for 2 to 3 minutes or until softened, stirring frequently.

While mushrooms are cooking, drizzle remaining 1 tablespoon oil evenly over pizza crusts. Spoon mushroom mixture evenly over crusts and crumble cheese over all. Bake directly on oven rack for 9 to 10 minutes or until hot and crust is golden brown. Remove from oven with a large spatula. Sprinkle with pepper to taste.

❧ *Serving suggestion:* Serve with a romaine salad tossed with balsamic vinaigrette.

HERBED FETA PIZZA

If fresh herbs are not available, substitute 1 teaspoon dried basil, 1 teaspoon dried oregano, and ¼ cup thinly sliced green onions with tops.

4 SERVINGS

½ cup pine nuts or coarsely chopped
   walnuts
4 thin slices small red onion
1 12-inch prepared pizza crust
4 ounces feta or goat cheese
Fresh basil, oregano, and chives
2 tablespoons olive oil
½ teaspoon bottled minced garlic

Heat oven to 450°F. Spread nuts on a small baking sheet and place in oven to toast for 6 minutes while oven preheats. While nuts are toasting, arrange onion rings evenly over pizza crust. Crumble cheese and sprinkle over crust. Chop enough herbs to equal ¼ cup and sprinkle over cheese. Sprinkle toasted nuts over herbs.

    Combine oil and garlic and drizzle evenly over pizza. Bake directly on oven rack for 8 to 10 minutes or until edges of pizza are golden brown. Slide a cookie sheet under the hot pizza to remove from oven. Cut into wedges.

✼ *Serving suggestion:* Serve with a fresh fruit salad.

PIZZA BREAD WITH PEPPERS AND ONIONS

Italian bread makes a thick, chewy crust for tasty, quick-cooking vegetables in this easy recipe.

4 SERVINGS

1 14-inch-long loaf Italian bread (about
    16 ounces)
¾ cup prepared pizza sauce
½ red bell pepper
½ yellow or green bell pepper
4 thin slices red onion
2 cups preshredded mozzarella cheese

Heat broiler with rack about 4 inches from heat source. Heat oven to 400°F. (If broiler and oven are one unit, change to oven temperature after bread is toasted.) Cut bread lengthwise in half and place on a large foil-lined baking sheet. Broil 2 minutes or until lightly toasted. Remove from broiler.

Spread pizza sauce evenly over bread, spreading to edges to prevent them from overbrowning. Cut red and yellow peppers into very thin slices and arrange over pizza sauce. Separate onion slices into rings and arrange over pepper strips. Sprinkle cheese evenly over all. Bake for 10 minutes or until cheese is melted. Cut into serving-size pieces.

❧ *Serving suggestion:* Serve with sliced tomatoes drizzled with balsamic vinaigrette and minced fresh basil leaves.

MEXICALI PIZZA

Pizza takes a cue from Mexican cuisine here, with tortillas as its "crust" and salsa as its flavorful sauce.

2 SERVINGS

2 10- to 12-inch flour tortillas
½ cup prepared mild or medium salsa or
 picante sauce
1 teaspoon ground cumin
1 16-ounce can black beans
2 large or 3 small green onions with tops
1½ cups preshredded Monterey Jack cheese
 or Cojack cheese
1 ripe avocado
Sour cream for garnish
Chopped cilantro for garnish, if desired

Heat broiler with rack about 6 inches from heat source. Place tortillas on a foil-lined baking sheet. Broil for 1 minute, turn, and broil second side for 1 minute or until lightly browned. Remove from broiler. Reset oven to 425°F.

Combine salsa and cumin and spread evenly over tortillas, spreading to edges. Drain and rinse beans and sprinkle evenly over salsa. Thinly slice green onions and sprinkle over beans. Top with cheese. Bake for 9 to 10 minutes. While tortillas are cooking, slice avocado. Place spoke-fashion over hot cooked tortillas. Cut into wedges and serve with sour cream and, if desired, cilantro.

🌿 *Serving suggestion:* Serve with sliced ripe papaya sprinkled with fresh lime juice.

SWISS PIZZA

If preshredded Swiss cheese is not available, tear 6 ounces of sliced Swiss cheese into pieces to cover toppings.

4 SERVINGS

1 6-ounce jar marinated artichoke hearts
1 12-inch prepared pizza crust
1 2¼-ounce can sliced ripe olives, drained
¼ cup chopped drained sun-dried
    tomatoes in oil
1½ cups preshredded Swiss cheese

Heat oven to 450°F. Drain artichoke hearts, reserving 2 table-spoons marinade. Drizzle marinade evenly over pizza crust. Coarsely chop artichoke hearts and sprinkle over pizza crust with olives and sun-dried tomatoes. Sprinkle cheese evenly over crust. Bake directly on oven rack for 9 to 10 minutes or until cheese is melted. Slide a cookie sheet under the hot pizza to remove from oven. Cut into wedges.

❧ *Serving suggestion:* Serve with coleslaw.

BAKED BEAN AND CHEDDAR PIZZA

This is a quite different take on the traditional pizza. It's easy and filling.

4 SERVINGS

1 cup bottled or canned baked beans,
    undrained
¼ teaspoon hot pepper sauce
1 12-inch prepared pizza crust
4 thin slices red onion
1½ cups preshredded sharp cheddar cheese

Heat oven to 450°F. Combine beans and pepper sauce and spoon evenly over pizza crust. Separate onion slices into rings and place over bean mixture. Sprinkle cheese evenly over pizza. Bake directly on oven rack for 9 to 10 minutes or until edges are golden brown and cheese is melted. Slide a cookie sheet under the hot pizza to remove from oven. Cut into wedges.

🌿 *Serving suggestion:* Serve with tomato soup.

Index

INDEX